KT-508-427

635.9674 QUI

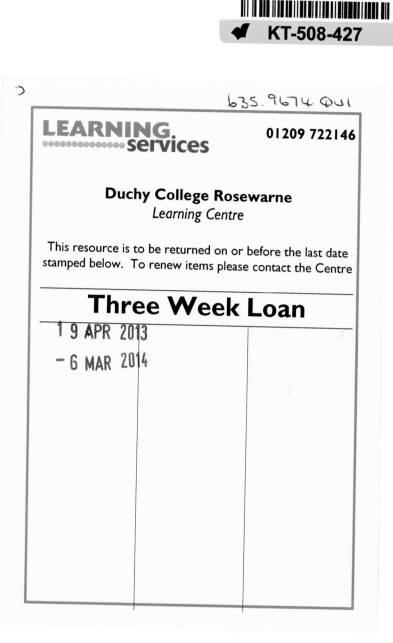

LEARNING.
•••••••••••••••services

01209 722146

Duchy College Rosewarne
Learning Centre

This resource is to be returned on or before the last date
stamped below. To renew items please contact the Centre

Three Week Loan

1 9 APR 2013

- 6 MAR 2014

RINGPRESS

DR003625

CORNWALL COLLEGE

Published by Ringpress Books,
A Division of Interpet Publishing
Vincent Lane, Dorking, Surrey RH4 3YX

© 2003 RINGPRESS BOOKS

ALL RIGHTS RESERVED

No part of this book may be reproduced or transmitted in any
form or by any means, electronic or mechanical, including
photocopying, recording, or by any information storage and
retrieval system, without permission in writing from the
Publisher.

ISBN 1 86054 222 0

Printed and bound by Bell & Bain Lt., Glasgow

10 9 8 7 6 5 4 3 2 1

CONTENTS

Orontium aquaticum; Potomageton crispus; Ranunculus aquatilis; Utricularia vulgaris); Water lilies (White water lilies; Yellow water lilies; Pink water lilies; Red water lilies; Unusual lily varieties; Planting water lilies); Floating plants (Eichhornia crassipes; Hydrocharis morsus-ranae; Lemna species; Pista straiotes; Rorippa nasturtium aquaticum; Stratiotes aloides; Trapa natans); Bog plants (Cardamine pratensis; Filipendula ulmaria; Gunnera manicata; Impatiens glandulifera; Iris kaempferi 'Rose Queen'; Lysimachia clethroides; Petasites officinalis; Potentilla palustris; Primula; Rheum palmatum; Rodgersia aesculifolia 'Batalin'; Schizostylis coccinea; Sisyrinchium species).

AUTHOR'S NOTE

While some people may disagree with my advice and opinions, my knowledge has been gathered, often the hard way, through my career as a fish farm employee, retail shop owner and in the sturgeon farm/consultancy business that I now run. My fishkeeping spans more than 24 years and I still have most of my original stock, so although my methods and ideas may differ from others, I feel my fish can vouch for these often opinionated views!

There are many people who have kept fish for two or three years and now consider themselves 'experts'. However, if you want good advice, go to a well-established retailer and listen carefully to what you are told. Fishkeeping is very much an 'It worked for me' hobby. If unsure, always seek professional advice – it could save you time, money and the lives of your fish.

Finally, I hope you enjoy fishkeeping and water gardening for as long as I have.

ACKNOWLEDGEMENTS

The author would like to thank Roger and Biddi Kings of Merebrook Water Plants for their help with Chapter Four: Planting the Pond. Thank you also to Dave Bevan, who provided some of the photography, and to Tetra UK.

INTRODUCTION

The purpose of this book is to set the fishkeeper/water gardener on the right track and keep him there by using tried-and-tested methods.

Water gardening is a wonderful hobby that not only gives enormous pleasure when finished, but also adds movement to any garden, however small. It brings in more wildlife, too – even some you may not want!

It has been said that an established water garden and pond requires less maintenance than an ordinary garden of the same size, but this is not an excuse to overlook any work needed in the day-to-day running of the feature.

Probably the most fascinating part of the feature is the water itself. In every season, it reflects the garden's changing pattern – not only literally. As the pond comes to life in spring, matures through the summer, and dies down in the autumn (fall) ready for the winter's hibernation, it creates its own world within your garden.

There are useful tips throughout the book, presented in special panels. These 'gems' have been culled from my own experiences, so read them in case you come across the same problems.

This is the general advice that I would offer to every would-be water gardener:

• **Preparation:** This is the key. The more time you spend getting everything ready for the work, the better and smoother the job will run and the better the final result will be.

• **Be patient.** Rushing it is the wrong way to build the perfect water garden. If you can't do something on your own, get some help.

• **Little and often.** Maintenance should be done as required, not left until something has gone wrong. Remember, this is supposed to be a hobby, not a chore.

• **Budget.** If you have to save a little, don't skimp on the major items such as liners, underlays, and underground cables. Instead, leave less important things, such as fountain ornaments, for another day.

CHAPTER 1

BUILDING THE POND

Once you have made the decision to add a pond to your garden, you must decide what type you want: waterfall, fountain or wildlife pond? Only you can answer this question. Write a list of the things you would like to see, and try to stick to one theme. For example, don't try to mix Japanese pergolas with formal brickwork.

Safety is the number one consideration if children are to be allowed near the pond. Always build it so that it is in view from the house, and consider a fence to avoid accidents.

Good planning is vital. It not only gives you an idea of the materials and costs involved, but will also help you to avoid expensive mistakes.

POSITIONING THE POND

The position can often be the deciding factor which makes the pond work or not, and it will cause problems at a later date if the incorrect site is chosen. Areas under trees should be avoided, as leaves will fall in and pollute small ponds in the autumn (fall). They will also clog pump filters.

WILDLIFE POND

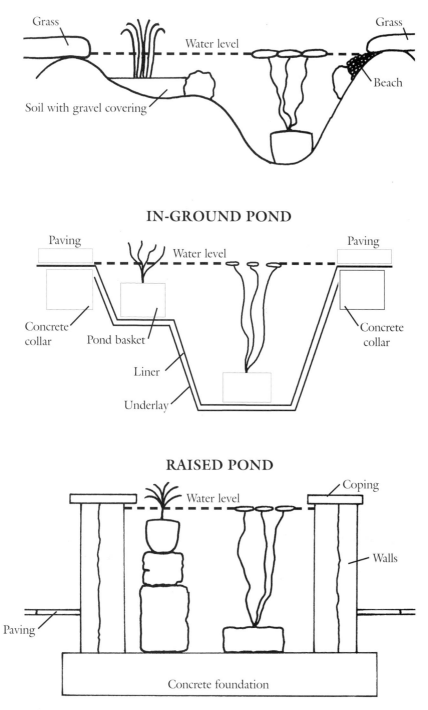

Grass

Grass

Water level

Soil with gravel covering

Beach

IN-GROUND POND

Paving

Paving

Water level

Concrete collar

Pond basket

Liner

Underlay

Concrete collar

RAISED POND

Coping

Water level

Walls

Paving

Concrete foundation

Plant roots can have many effects on the pond and its surrounding structures. Some plants can puncture pond liners, lift moulded liners, and crack paved areas. Plants that need special care, such as fruit trees or roses, must be planted away from the pond as any sprays could affect your fish and plants.

If the garden has poorly draining soil, it is best not to build the pond in the lowest part of the garden. Water will collect here during wet periods and may flood the pond and possibly contaminate it. A flood may even lift the liner and empty the pond and contents on to the surrounding ground.

As water finds its own level, a flat site is the easiest place to build. Ponds can be built on sloping ground but extra precautions need to be taken to strengthen the downhill banks to avoid a disaster. Large rocks or extra-deep concrete collars can be used to strengthen the bank.

Areas that are windswept should be avoided, as excess evaporation in summer and excessive cooling in winter can be a major problem, especially for the plants. A small windbreak or low hedge around the pond will help to alleviate the problem.

Before digging, always check to ensure that no household supplies (such as gas, electricity or waste water drainage) run in the area where the pond is to go. Don't build the pond close to the house or a garden wall as the digging could cause subsidence. If the pond has to be close to a house or building, it is advisable to check with a structural engineer.

Avoid placing ponds near roads or public paths as fumes from vehicles can cause harm to the fish, and, if the pond can be seen, it makes an easy target for thieves.

Consider the cost of getting electricity and water to the pond when choosing a site. Easy access will save money.

Total shade all day will stop most water plants from flowering, but it also controls algae growth. For a fish-only pond, full shade is acceptable. The downside is low summer water temperature, which will slow the fishes' growth and can lead to poor resistance to disease.

Full sun is good for plants but can create large algae growth problems, and, in warmer climates, excessive water temperatures, which will in turn lower the oxygen content, which could result in suffocating the fish.

The ideal position for a pond is in semi-shade with about six hours of sun per day. Early morning and late afternoon sun is the best. It avoids the hottest part of the day, but still gives enough light to encourage the water lilies to flower.

Take into account the reaction from neighbours, as the sound of a rushing torrent might not be their idea of a tranquil evening in the garden. If possible, design the waterfall with a by-pass if this could be a concern.

SIZE

Always try to build the largest pond that you can fit into the space available, as the larger the pool, the greater the water volume, and the easier it is to balance and maintain. If planting the pond, find out the correct levels and depths for the shelves that the plants will sit on. If planting water lilies, allow 2 square metres (21.5 square feet) of surface area per plant for them to flourish.

Small ponds of 2 cubic metres (70.5 cubic feet) or less require constant care and can become a chore rather than a hobby. Larger ponds of 5 cubic metres (176.5 cubic feet) or more are a great deal less work and little maintenance is required.

DEPTH

For the average garden pond, 60 cm (2 feet) is the minimum depth and 75 cm (2 feet, 6 inches) or more is ideal. In colder climates, 100 cm (3 feet, 4 inches) should be the minimum and 120 cm (4 feet) is ideal. Depths greater than 150 cm (5 feet) should be left to the koi keepers, as a very deep pond is very slow to warm up in the spring. This reduces the time when the fish can grow, and smaller fish will spend most of their time in deeper water out of view, where they also feel safer.

There are many reasons that koi keepers give for having deep ponds of 2 metres (6 feet) or more. Some claim the greater depth gives the fish a better body shape and that the fish grow better. Fish producers and farmers disagree, as their growing-on ponds are nearly always shallow, except in warm countries.

The main reasons for poor body shape are:
- **Poor food:** fatty foods create fat fish.
- **Environment:** lack of oxygen and poor water quality will stop the fish metabolising the food to best advantage, which can

create underweight fish or stunted growth of the skeleton.
- **Genetics:** if the parent fish have a poor body shape, there is a good chance the offspring will have similar problems.

SHAPE

The easiest ponds to build are rectangular, but this is not a popular shape, as it does not blend into many garden schemes. To make lining easy, it is best to avoid small radius corners and too many planting shelves of different depths. Complex shapes, such as figures of eight, are attractive to look at but difficult and expensive to line. Ponds can be built with just three depths – one for the marginals, one for the deepwater aquatics, and the last for the base and water lilies.

If the sides slope into the base about 2 cm (0.75 inches) for every 30-cm (1-foot) depth, this will help the sides to stay put while the pond is dug, and also to allow the ice to force its way up rather than to split the pond. In sandy soil, the sides will need to be less steep, to stop the walls collapsing.

Wildlife ponds need a shallow 'beach' to allow the amphibians to climb in and out, and to allow uninvited guests to escape if they fall in. The shallow sides can also assist predatory animals to fish more effectively, so tall plants around the edge will be necessary to protect the pond life.

BUILDING METHODS

There is a range of different methods for waterproofing a pond. Most are reliable, but some are more difficult and costly to install.

The easiest and most reliable method is to use a sheet of liner. There are many types on the market, but the most popular is PVC (polyvinyl chloride). It is a very flexible and pliable material with life expectancy of up to 35 years, and is easy to shape and install. It is simple to repair and good value for money.

The minimum thickness is 0.5 mm (0.2 inches) for small to medium ponds, and 0.8 mm (0.3 inches) for medium to large ponds. If you intend to use large, heavy rockery stones, you can purchase a 1-mm-thick (0.4-inch-thick) material, which is very strong and resists punctures very well, but can be difficult to lay if the shape is complicated.

The oldest and best-known liner is butyl, a rubber-like synthetic material. It is very flexible and ideal for all projects from the smallest to the largest. It is also good for the more complex shapes, and can be heat welded, though this is best left to a professional. Repairs are easy with either a mastic tape or liquid butyl glue, and it has a very long life expectancy of up to 50 years.

Pre-formed ponds are ideal for raised ponds or sites where the use of liners would be unsuitable, such as in very stony ground or where abundant roots could cause punctures.

Of the materials used to make pre-formed ponds, fibre glass is by far the best. It is very strong and resilient, but it is produced in a comparatively small number of sizes and shapes. Simple installations can be done in a weekend. Pre-formed ponds can also be made from a vacuum-formed plastic shell. These are cheaper, but more difficult to install as they have no inherent rigidity, making the preparation work more important to achieve a satisfactory finish. The most expensive pre-formed ponds are made from fibre rock, which is a mixture of glass fibre and concrete. It is the most natural-looking pond material, but there are few shapes available and large ponds are very heavy.

Finally, you can build your pond from concrete. It is the most difficult and expensive method, but it will last the longest if properly done. However, I would not recommend it for novices.

GROUND-LEVEL PONDS

LINER PONDS

If you plan to set your pond in paving, it will need a concrete 'collar' around it. Use a garden hose or rope to outline the pond's basic shape, then start to dig around the *outside* of the hose/rope for the collar. It needs to be as wide as the paving you intend to lay and 15 to 20 cm (6 to 8 inches) deep. The less stable (i.e. sandy) the soil, the deeper the collar needs to be. If the collar is very deep or wide, reinforcing mesh can be added. You will eventually fill this trench with concrete, leaving room at the top for your paving slabs and a mortar bed in which to set them.

Pegs need to be hammered into the ground around the inside of the trench to the height of the bottom of the mortar bed, to give you an accurate guide when laying the concrete. As each peg is hammered in, it can be levelled with a straight edge from

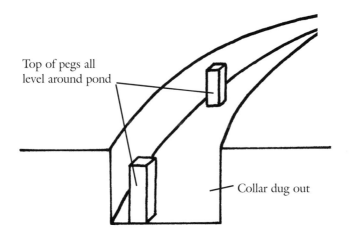

Top of pegs all
level around pond

Collar dug out

the last peg. Place as many as necessary to complete a set
around the trench (see above figure).

Before the concrete is laid, remember to allow for an electrical
conduit and overflow pipe and/or a water supply pipe. A large-
diameter pipe can be laid under the collar to allow all supplies to
pass through in one area, or smaller conduits can be laid for each
supply.

With all pegs level, a ready-mix concrete can be laid into the
trench, or a mix of one part cement to four parts ballast. Lay all the
concrete in one go, as joins will be weaker than the rest and could
cause the collar to break. With the concrete laid, water in and level
off, but leave a rough surface so the mortar holding the paving can
stick to it. This in turn will help to prevent the paving becoming
loose.

When the concrete is dry, start to dig out the main pond area.
For the first planting shelf you will need to dig to a depth of 20 to
25 cm (8 to 10 inches). This will be deep enough for most
marginals, but if you intend to grow larger plants, make the shelf a
little deeper to allow for larger planting baskets.

Mark out the shelves to a width of 25 to 30 cm (10 to 12
inches) and dig out the rest of the pond to a minimum depth of 60
cm (2 feet). The sides need to be sloped to stop them collapsing
inwards when the pond is emptied. You need to allow a minimum
of 10 cm (4 inches) for every 30 cm (1 foot) of depth.

The base of the pond needs to be flat to give a crease-free finish when the liner is installed, but with a slight slope to a sump, so that the water can be pumped out quickly and easily when you want to drain the pond and clean it. Check the excavation for any stones or roots that may damage the liner, and remove them.

> *Tip: The better the preparation the better the finish, so spend time now to ensure the excavation is just as you want it. Once the liner is in, it will be very difficult, if not impossible, to rectify any problems.*

Once the excavation is complete, measure lengthways for the liner size using a tape measure or length of string. Run the tape from halfway across the collar down the side of the pond, across the base, up the other side, and halfway across the collar again. Do this two to three times and use the longest measurement. Follow the same procedure to find the width, then, armed with the sizes, purchase a liner and underlay to fit. If you cannot get the exact size, go larger not smaller. Liners do not stretch to fit despite what some manufactures would have you believe! Buy a good-quality underlay – builders' polythene and similar plastic sheets are not good enough. A non-woven mat is the best kind, and will last the life of the liner.

> *Tip: Many liner manufacturers' guarantees are only valid if an underlay is used, so check this out when you purchase your liner.*

Lay the underlay across the pond and overlap each piece by 7 to 10 cm (3 to 4 inches) to stop stones or roots penetrating through any gaps. Once the underlay is in place, water it. This makes it heavier and will prevent it moving when you drag the liner over it. Wait until the liner is in place before you trim off any excess.

The liner should be unfolded on the lawn and checked before you lay it. There is no point laying a liner with a hole in it! If possible, choose a warm day, as PVC liners are less pliable when cold. Spreading out the liner on the lawn will warm it up and make it more flexible, so it will fit in and finish more easily.

You will need one person at each corner to lift the liner, carry it over the pond, and lower it over the hole. With one end halfway over the collar, start to push the liner into the shape and fit it as best you can. Once it is in place, start to fill the pond with water. Use a water meter if you can, as it will be useful later to know the pond's volume for treatments and filter sizes.

When there is a 10-cm (4-inch) depth of water in the pond, pull the liner to get the base as smooth and crease-free as possible, and, as the level rises, fold the liner to fit the pond. Larger folds can be fixed in place with mastic tape or a glue suitable for your pond liner. Check the type with your supplier.

Fill the pond to the top and complete any folds and pleats. If you let the liner settle for a few hours, the weight of the water will make sure the liner fits into all the shelves and the shape of the pond. Next, trim the liner and underlay so that both cover only half of the collar.

Use a mortar mix, with waterproofing added, and lay the paving around the pond. It should slope away from the pond, about 0.5 cm per 30 cm (0.25 inches per foot), to stop rainwater running in from the surrounding lawn or flower beds.

Tip: To get an even slope on the paving around the pond, tape a small piece of wood on to the level to give a 0.5 cm per 30 cm (0.25 inches per foot) fall. With the wood in place, you will get an even measurement each time you use it and a matching fall around the pond.

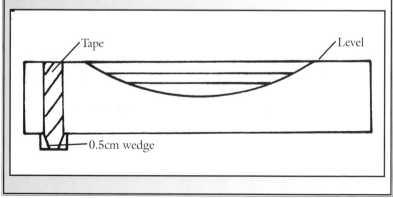

Leave the mortar to dry for 24 hours, to ensure the slabs do not move while you work on the pointing.

Again, use a mortar mix with waterproofing and start to point the paving, pushing the mortar right into the gaps to ensure there are no air pockets. Otherwise, if water gets into these in winter and freezes, it will crack the pointing.

Other edging methods include:
• Timber
• Stone or rocks
• Soil
• Grass
• Brickwork
• Liner with pebbles stuck on it.

PRE-FORMED POND LINERS

Before deciding which pre-formed pond to purchase, get a catalogue showing the sizes and shapes available. Then you can measure out each pond design in the area you have set aside for it and see which will fit in with your plan and make best use of the area. Select the largest pond that will fit into the space. The deeper the pond, the better. Small, shallow ponds may freeze completely in very cold weather unless you fit a heater.

INSTALLATION

If the pond is large and heavy, you will need help, otherwise you risk damaging it – or yourself!

Position the pond in its final place and mark the ground around the outside of the deepest level. Dig out an area 10 to 15 cm (4 to 6 inches) larger on each side than the marked area to allow for back-filling when the pond is installed. The hole needs to be the maximum depth of the pond plus 10 cm (4 inches), which will allow for a sand base.

Lower the pond into the hole and mark around the rest of it. As before, dig out to 10 to 15cm (4 to 6 inches) wider than the mark and 10 cm (4 inches) deeper. If the pond has more levels, continue until the edge of the pond is below the finished paving level, allowing for the mortar bed and thickness of slab or edging material on top of this.

Once you have dug the hole, check all over for stones or tree roots and remove them. Cover the base and shelved areas with sand or sieved soil and rake to a level finish.

Lower the pond into the hole without knocking the sand off the shelves. With a straight-edged piece of wood and a level, check across the pond width and length to ensure the pond is level in the hole. This may not be possible at this stage with a flexible plastic type.

Once the pond is level, put 15 cm (6 inches) of water into the bottom to anchor it while you back-fill around the outside with sand or sieved soil. If the pond starts to lift, add more water to increase the weight. Pack down the sand so that it is firm, and then finish filling the pond with water.

If you are going to put paving around the edge of the pond, you will need to dig a trench for a concrete foundation. This should be the width of your paving and a depth of 15 to 20 cm (6 to 8 inches) all around the pond. You will need to lay an electrical conduit to the pond at this stage if you are going to have a pump.

Lay a mix of one part cement to four parts ballast. Finish off to the same level as the lip of the pre-formed pond.

If the pond is made from flexible plastic material, you will have to do the final levelling at this point by putting extra sand under the lower edges to raise them, or by removing excess sand to make high edges lower. Once the concrete has set, the paving can be laid.

CONCRETE PONDS

These are harder work than any other type and far more costly, but you are not restricted to shape or size and the finish is excellent. Nevertheless, it is a job for the DIY expert or the professional water gardener.

With newer waterproofing agents, it is possible to construct a pond without having to render it to make it watertight, although rendering can give a better finish.

There are two methods for the construction of concrete ponds. The free-formed method gives the most natural look and it is the best for wildlife ponds or plant-based ponds. The other method is for formal ponds and involves using shuttering and reinforcing steel.

THE FREE-FORMED METHOD

This method is not suitable for larger ponds on soft, moving soils such as clay. Due to the nature of clay soils, the constant movement from wet winter to dry summer can cause the concrete to split or break the pond's back by lifting it out of the ground. If you need to use this method on clay, you will need to lay extensive drainage to keep ground water from the pond area, and reinforcing will also be needed.

You will need to allow for the thickness of the concrete in your measurements when designing the pond. For example, with a small pond you will need to add an extra 20 cm (8 inches) – 2 x 10 cm (2 x 4 inches) – to each dimension and 15 cm (6 inches) to the depth. Dig a trench to take conduit and other pipes that may be required, such as a water supply or overflow.

Dig the pond to the chosen size and line the hole with a damp-proof membrane or cheap pond liner. This stops the ground drying the concrete out too quickly and cracking it. The sides of the pond will have to be gently sloping, otherwise the concrete will not stay in place once it has been laid.

Mix your concrete using one part cement to four parts ballast with added waterproofing. Reinforcing glass fibre can be added as it is mixed, which improves the finished strength of the surface and reduces hairline cracks as the concrete dries. For small ponds, mixing yourself is fine, but for larger projects it may be cheaper and more convenient to arrange for ready-mixed concrete to be delivered.

It is best to lay all the concrete in one day, to reduce the number of joints and therefore the chance of a leak. If this is not possible, leave a rough edge for the join as this will give a better surface on which to key the new concrete.

Tamp down the concrete to get all the air pockets out and use a trowel to smooth the surface. If the mix is very wet, allow the concrete to dry for 15 to 30 minutes before doing this. Smooth the surface as many times as is necessary to get the best finish. Keeping the trowel clean will help, as, when the surface approaches drying, it will become very difficult to get a clean finish. The more you try, the more mess you are likely to make. Stop as soon as you see this happen. Leave a level, rough surface around the top of the pond, to act as a key for the paving (see chapter two).

CONCRETE POND WITH SHUTTERING

This method is suitable only for regular-shaped ponds. When designing the pond, the sides need to slope outwards to some degree, otherwise, when ice forms in the winter, it will expand and crack the concrete shell.

Dig out the pond and compact the soil on the base and sides. Cover the excavation with polythene or a cheap liner, to stop the concrete drying too quickly. Place the reinforcing metalwork across the base and up the sides, but stop 5 cm (2 inches) below the finished height to ensure the metalwork is well covered in concrete and cannot rust. The frame needs to be held 5 cm (2 inches) off the base and sides. Use small pieces of rock as spacers to stop the reinforcing protruding from the concrete.

Mix, or use a ready-mixed concrete with a waterproofing agent to cover the base, tamp to remove air pockets, and trowel smooth. Allow to dry for two days. If the weather is warm, cover it with polythene to slow down the process.

Build shuttering for the sides from thick plywood cut to size, and paint a releasing agent on to the wood surface so that it can be removed easily from the concrete. The shuttering will need to be braced very well against the opposite side to stop it moving. Rounded ends can be formed by bending thin plywood around a curved form, and bracing very securely.

Important Note: Concrete can weigh up to 2,800 kgs (2.8 tonnes) per cubic metre (176 lbs per cubic foot). Therefore, the bracing needs to be very strong. If you are unsure, get a professional to check it or build it for you.

Mix the concrete to a wet consistency with waterproofing agent, and pour the mix evenly around the shuttering. Watch carefully – if the forms move, it will require some quick work to stop a disaster. Fill to the top of the shuttering and vibrate with a vibrating poker to eliminate all the air bubbles and make sure all the voids are filled.

Allow the concrete to dry for seven to ten days before removing the forms. Keep the pond surface moist with a water spray and allow to dry slowly over two to three weeks. This will give a very strong concrete. A render 2 to 3 cm (1 to 1.5 inches) thick may be necessary if the shuttering has left marks or if there are gaps. This should be left to dry for five to seven days before filling with water.

Any pond in which concrete or cement-based products come into contact with water should be filled up at least twice before any livestock, including plants, are introduced. It is advisable to pre-paint with a neutralising agent all surfaces that could affect the water.

> *Tip: There are many products available and some require new surfaces that have been allowed to dry for up to eight weeks before painting, so read the label carefully. Rushing may prove expensive in the long run.*

Always check the pH (acidity) of the water once the pond is filled. If it rises to more than pH9, it could be that the cement is dissolving in the water, which will affect the fish and plants. If so, it needs to be remedied before any livestock is placed in the pond.

RAISED PONDS

The basic construction involves more work than a ground-level pond, but raised ponds have many advantages:

• They involve less digging, and, therefore, there is less spoil to remove, reducing costs.
• A raised pond will stay cleaner, as less dust and leaves will blow in. Therefore, less maintenance is required.
• They offer better protection from predators, as access is more difficult.
• They provide added seating for the garden and a place from which to feed your fish.

As with ground-level ponds, you can use pre-formed, flexible liners or concrete.

PRE-FORMED LINERS

This is the simplest to install. Once the liner is in its final position, mark around the outside of the top lip, using a level in the vertical position to ensure that you don't make the walled area too small. Remove the pond, and the outline left is the minimum size

RAISED PONDS

FORMAL LINER

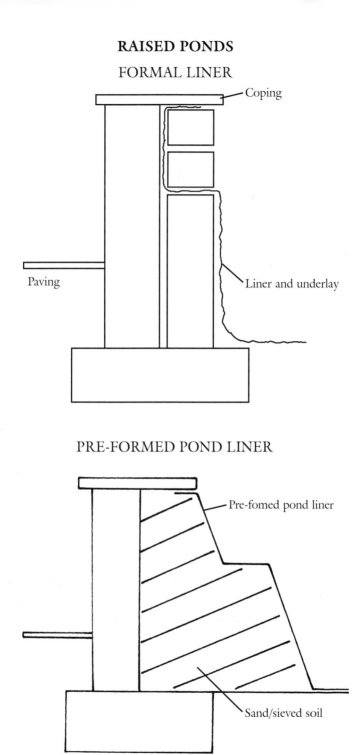

Coping

Paving

Liner and underlay

PRE-FORMED POND LINER

Pre-fomed pond liner

Sand/sieved soil

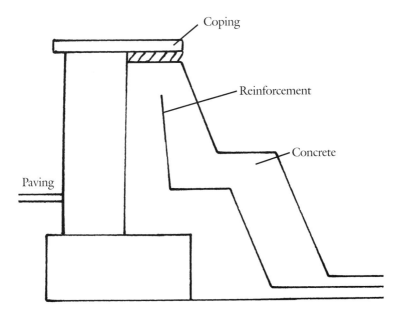

required. If you are going to enclose the filter or a garden area as well, remember to make room for it all.

Once the area is marked out, dig a foundation for the wall. The top of the foundation needs to be lower than the bottom of the pond for added safety. For small walls up to 60 cm (2 feet) high, a foundation 30 cm by 30 cm (1 foot by 1 foot) should be sufficient. On sandy soil, it will be better to build a larger foundation. Use a four to one, ballast-to-cement mix, and lay the foundation. Level all the way around and allow to dry for one to two days.

Dig out any soil that is needed to install the pond, allowing for a 5-cm (2-inch) sand base. With the pond in position, build the wall to the required height making sure it is level. Allow to dry for two to three days.

Tip: It is not important to build the wall to exactly the correct height, as the bricks may not fit. You can adjust the pond's height to suit, putting extra sand under it to raise it, or less to lower it.

With the wall finished and the pond installed to the correct height and level, check the pond and begin filling it with water. As the water rises, back-fill around the edge with sand, packing it as you go. Stop before you reach the top so that you can install any cables or overflow pipes that are required.

Once all the services are in place, the back-filling can be completed. Tamp down as firmly as possible without moving the pond, leave a few centimetres (an inch or two) below the pond lip, and fill with mortar to give an extra area for the coping to bond to.

FLEXIBLE LINERS

Mark out the area to be used for the pond and add the thickness of the walls to the dimensions. For small, shallow ponds up to 90 cm (3 feet) deep, a 75-mm (0.3-inch), concrete-block-built inner wall, and a decorative outer wall, will be sufficient.

Dig the foundations large enough to accommodate the two walls, so that the foundation is below the base of the pond. The foundation should be about 40 cm (16 inches) wide and 30 cm (1 foot) deep. Build the two walls using wall ties to increase the strength, up to 20 cm (8 inches) from the finished height. Build the outer wall up to its final height. Let the walls dry for three to four days. Run any cables or pipes that are necessary in the cavity between the two walls.

Installing the liner at this point will help to disguise it from view. Cover the pond with underlay so that it covers all the walls and base and overlaps down between the two walls. Make sure it fits well, as any creases will be seen through the liner when the pond is full.

Tip: If the pond is in an exposed site, you can line it with 25-mm-thick (1-inch-thick) polystyrene insulation sheets and then put the underlay over the top to hold it in place and cover the joins. This will prevent the pond temperature from fluctuating in windy weather.

Lay the liner in the hole and fit as best you can. Start to fill the pond, fold the liner as the water rises and pull any creases out of the base. When the water is 5 cm (2 inches) from the top of the inner wall, stop filling.

Fixing the liner is a slow and difficult job, so help may be required on a large liner. Fold back the liner and underlay, and place a thin layer of wet mortar on the top of the inner wall. Fold the underlay on top of this, then place another layer of mortar on the underlay and fold the liner over it.

With a stiff mortar mix, with added waterproofing agent, lay the next course of bricks (or decorative blocks or stone) and bring the liner up behind. Lay the next course and then fold the liner over the top of the inner wall towards the pond. Let this dry for one to two days. In the case of larger ponds, it is best to fill the cavity between the walls with a concrete mix to increase the strength. Trim the liner so that it covers only half of the inner wall, run any conduit over the edge and into the pond.

Next, place a thin layer of mortar under the liner and fold it back over the inner wall. Lay mortar on top of the liner and on the front wall and lay the coping/wall cap across both, with a slight slope away from the pond. This will stop water running across the coping into the pond. Continue around the whole pond, and let the mortar dry before pointing the coping.

CONCRETE PONDS

Dig out the required depth and tamp the base flat to reduce any soil movement. Try to get a level finish across the base, leaving a deeper area for a sump so that it is possible to drain the pond for cleaning when needed. Dig a deeper trench around the edge where the wall is to stand. This will act as a more stable outer foundation.

As with the other raised ponds, the outer wall is built on foundations. It is also part of the concrete base or raft in this case. Reinforcing steel needs to be placed so that it comes up inside the pond close to the wall. The shuttering needs to be strong to hold the concrete in place and the outer wall needs to be dry so that it does not move when you pour the concrete into the shuttering. Use releasing agent on the shuttering.

With the shuttering in place and before pouring the concrete, insert any conduits or pipes and cover the ends with site caps or heavy duty tape, to stop them becoming blocked with concrete.

Using a wet concrete mix with waterproofing agent, pour the concrete level with the top of the outer wall. Use a vibrating poker to eliminate air bubbles from the concrete. Try not to leave long

ROSEWARNE
LEARNING CENTRE

periods between batches of concrete, as this can lead to leaks and weak areas. Leave the concrete to dry for seven to ten days before removing the shuttering. Keep the concrete moist by spraying for two to three weeks after removal to allow it to cure slowly.

Any marks or damaged areas need to be repaired before the final filling. If you intend to paint the pond, you can mix some of the paints with sand to use as a filler. For deep holes, make a thicker mix. Paint several normal coats over the top once dry, and allow to soak in. If the concrete is laid correctly, you should have a finish good enough to use without applying a render.

RENDERING

If you require a very smooth finish, or if the pond shows signs of leaking, the only choice is to render it.

Preparation is the key to getting the best finish with a render. Brush down the surface to remove any dust or loose material and paint over the pond with PVA solution to help provide a key for the render. The mix is one part cement to four parts fine sand, mixed with a waterproofing agent.

If a thick render is needed, it is best to do it in several thin layers as they will dry better and be easier to apply. To reinforce the render, add glass fibre to the mix. This stops any cracks spreading and may prevent the underlying structure from cracking if it dries too quickly.

The longer any concrete surface takes to dry, the harder the surface will be. Covering the render with wet hessian sacking will help to slow the curing process and give a very hard surface which will last for many years.

CHAPTER 2

EDGING
THE POND

O nce the pond has been lined, the edging can be added. There are a number of different styles, depending on the overall design of the pond. However, the materials used must meet a number of very important criteria before they can be considered for the job.

- The material must be non-toxic to all flora and fauna. Any fungus treatment or preservative impregnated in the material must be totally safe. If the supplier is unsure, it is best avoided.
- The material must not affect the water chemistry. For example, if soft limestone is used for paving, it will dissolve when acid rain falls on it and some will find its way into the pond. It could raise the pH to unacceptable levels.
- Any raw concrete products, such as concrete blocks or paving slabs, must be painted with sealer to stop the lime dissolving in the water.
- The material must not deteriorate or rot, as it would then need replacing. This is not always possible and, in any case, it would prove to be expensive.

PAVING

The most common way of edging is to pave around the pond, so that it is practical to walk around, to look at, and to work on, the pond. With a liner installed and a concrete collar, adding basic edging around the pond is easy. We have covered this in chapter one. Remember, the paving needs to be added when the pond is full and the water has pulled the liner into all the folds and ledges. If it is done with the pond empty, the weight of water when it is filled can pull the liner down, either tearing it or pulling the paving into the pond.

WALL POND

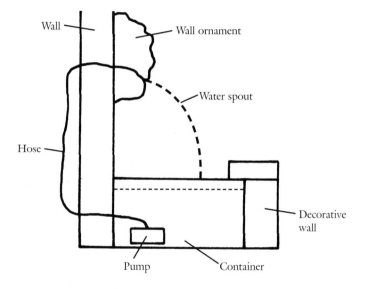

All slabs and surfaces around the pond must slope away from it to stop rainwater or any other material from flowing in. The edges of mortar nearest the pond need to be painted with waterproofing to protect fish and plants from the lime content, and to stop the water dissolving the mortar and weakening the edging.

GRASS EDGING

In less formal gardens, it is possible to run grass right up to the water to hide the edge of the pond. The liner needs to run under the grass for at least 30 cm (1 foot) to stop it pulling back into the

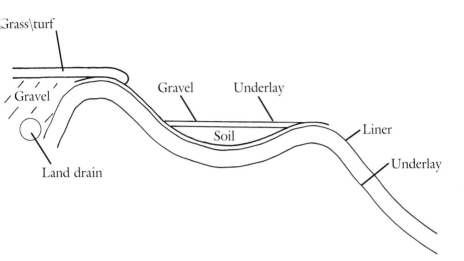

pond. You can use small treated stakes to hold the liner if the overlap is too short to hold on its own. Using underlay over the top of the liner not only protects it from plant roots, but also gives the grass something to root to.

However, there are a number of difficulties in running grass to the edge of the pond. The turf will act like a wick, and draw water out of the pond, lowering the level. This will mean a regular water top-up unless an auto top-up system is installed at the time of building. This could be expensive if you are on a water meter.

Grass will grow into the pond and across the surface if not controlled and cut regularly, and, as the water supply is plentiful, the growth will need weekly maintenance. It will not be possible to treat the surrounding lawn with chemicals, such as lawn feed or moss killer, as they could find their way into the pond and kill any wildlife or fish.

In areas of high rainfall or poor ground drainage, it may be necessary to place a drain around the pond to stop excess water from entering and causing it to overflow. A simple 'French' drain around the perimeter will normally be enough to remove the water.

It is essential that excess water is taken from around the pond as it can lead to the liner being forced to the water surface by the ground water pressure.

ROCKERY STONE

One of the best and neatest finishes is a well-laid-out rock edge. Unfortunately, it is also the easiest to mess up.

Before buying rock for a pond, you need to check that it does not dissolve. If the rock is very soft, such as tufa rock, it will upset the water chemistry. Some of the lava rocks available are not only very sharp, but also contain iron and other chemicals that can discolour the water or attack the metal in pond pumps. The most important thing to remember is that rock should only come from recognised quarries or collecting areas. A large quantity of rock is regularly stolen from areas of natural beauty. Do not encourage or aid this practice.

If the use of natural rock is not possible or desirable, you can buy fake rock made from a cement and fibre glass mix, or just plain fibre glass. It will be more expensive than natural rock, but it is lighter to use and easier to get home. The main drawback is the lack of different sizes and shapes, so more planning may be required to get a realistic effect.

Here are a few tips to make the rockwork more realistic:

- The strata (the lines of material that have been compressed to form the rock) should all run horizontally, as this is how it would be found naturally. Using rocks the wrong way up is the most common mistake in rockwork and it stands out like a sore thumb.
- Keep the edges smooth. You rarely see sharp edges on rocks in water, as they are worn smooth by the constant flow. Sharp edges of any kind are dangerous as the fish may damage themselves.
- Try not to use rocks of the same size and shape, as this is also unnatural.
- Never mix rock types.

Laying a rock edge takes more planning than when using other materials. First you need to build a collar, similar to the one for paving. This not only provides a firm base for the rockwork to fix to, but will also hold the soil back around the pond and allow weight to be placed on the edge without rocks falling into the pond.

When the pond is dug, lay the underlay over the collar and up over the surrounding soil, then lay the liner over in the same way.

ROCK EDGING

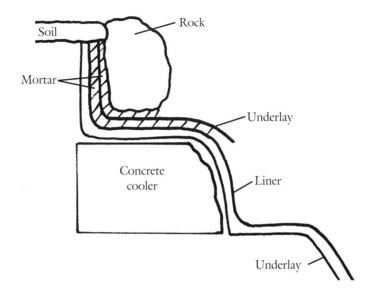

Place a thin layer of mortar on to the liner, then some underlay to protect the liner from the rock, then a thicker layer of mortar in which to bed the rock. Firm down the rock and fill the void behind it. This process will bond the rocks together, forming a stronger edge. When filling the gaps, try not to let the mortar show from the front. You can embed smaller rocks into the mortar, to make it less visible.

Note: To bed the rocks, use a three parts sand to one part cement mix with waterproofing agent in it. Make sure it is not too wet or mortar may run into the pond. It needs to be strong as you are sticking it to the liner.

BIRD'S EYE VIEW

Mortar fills gaps to strengthen rock edge.

BUILDING A BEACH

A beach is ideal for a wildlife pond as it provides a perfect area for animals to enter and leave the water. The pond needs to be built with a gentle slope up to the edge. The underlay and liner need to be run under the grass and secured either by laying turf on top of them, or with a stake. A top cover of underlay will stop the beach pebbles and plant roots damaging the liner. The underlay needs to run up the inside of the wall, as the wall needs to be mortared directly to the liner.

Once this is in place, a small retaining wall needs to be built at the beach end to stop the pebbles falling on to the pond base. The wall should finish between 3 cm (1 inch) and 5 cm (2 inches) below the water surface. This will stop larger fish digging up the beach, but will allow animals that fall into the pond to escape.

BEACH

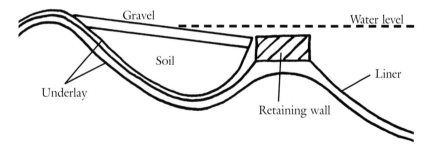

If plants are to be grown in the beach, a good layer of aquatic soil will be needed, before covering the whole surface with a thick layer of rounded gravel 10mm to 20mm in diameter.

> Tip: When planting a new beach, mix charcoal in with the soil. This will stop the soil from going 'off' until the new plants are established.

You can also make a beach by building a shallow trough around the top of the pond, to allow a larger planting area, instead of using planting baskets. This method is very popular in Europe, but it has major drawbacks compared to using planting baskets. The strongest plants take over the planting area and it is impossible to remove them cleanly from the pond as the planting material is not contained. Cleaning out the pond is very difficult, as the trough holds all the dirt and this cannot be washed out unless all the plants and media are removed. This means a lot of extra work.

TURF EDGE

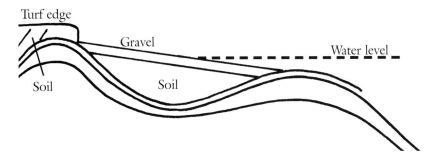

WOOD EDGING

Using wood around the pond has become increasingly popular as wood preservatives have become fish- and wildlife-friendly. One of the most common ways to edge in wood is to use railway sleepers. You should use new sleepers, which are available from suppliers, because used ones will have been treated with creosote, which is not fauna-friendly. The first sleeper can be fixed in place by drilling all the way through with a large-diameter drill (minimum of 10 mm or 0.4 inches). A length of reinforcing bar can be hammered into the ground below to secure the sleeper in place.

Next, the underlay needs to be laid over the sleeper, and then the liner, followed by a covering of underlay. Then lower the next sleeper on top of the first. The underlay and liner need to be pulled up the back of the sleepers so that the surface of the water comes halfway up the top one, to hide the liner. Secure the two sleepers together by hammering a post of treated wood in behind them, taking care to avoid damaging the liner. When the post is 50 mm (2 inches) below the top of the sleeper, secure it with long, corrosion-resistant screws. Three or four posts will be needed per sleeper to ensure that they are stable enough to walk on.

In some circumstances, it may be necessary to secure the lower sleeper as well. To do this without a leak occurring, use a good-quality sealing mastic between the post and the liner. As the screws are tightened up, the mastic will seal the hole.

> *Note: The mastic sealer must be fungicide-free, otherwise it is very toxic to fish.*

DECKING

Using decking instead of paving around the pond is a quick and simple way to provide an edge, although it may limit the shapes you can achieve.

DECKING AS AN EDGE

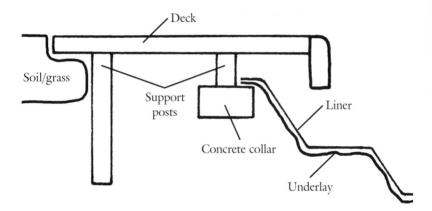

With the basic pond built, the decking will rest on the collar around the pond and on support posts. It is best not to let the edge of the deck touch the pond, as water will soak into the wood, discolouring it and allowing algae to grow on the damp surface. As long as the overhang is at least 75 mm (3 inches), it will hide the liner from view. Like paving, the deck should slope away, so that surface water does not run into the pond.

OVERHANGING THE POND

Decking over the pond is a good way of providing shade and protection from predators for the fish. It also offers a place for the pump and pipework to be sited out of view.

Securing the deck over the pond can be a problem, but there are three simple ways to achieve a safe, usable deck:
The easiest is over formal ponds that have a good, level paved or bricked edge, which will serve as a foundation for the deck.

POND DECKING

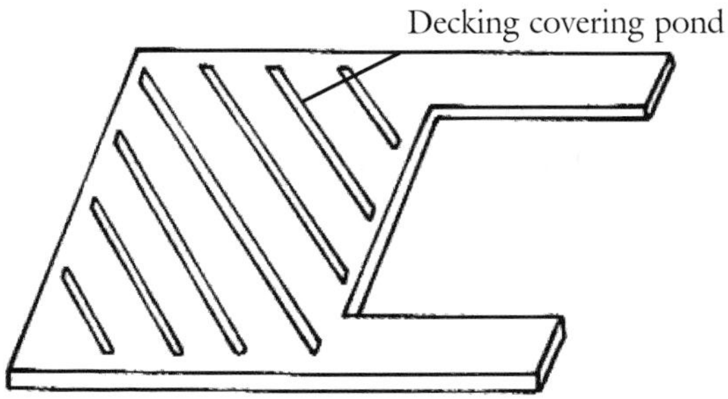

Decking covering pond

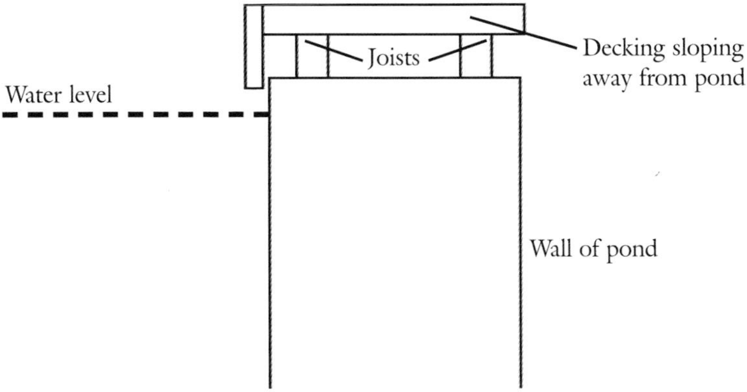

Decking sloping away from pond

Joists

Water level

Wall of pond

A simple deck resting on the edging offers the advantage of being removable, allowing maintenance to be carried out when necessary, but obviously, it offers no edge as such for the pond.

A more complex but easy design allows a deck to overhang the pond. The overhang or unsupported part of the deck should be no more than 25 per cent of the width of the deck, to a maximum of 1 metre (3 feet). For example, if a deck is 3 metres (10 feet) wide, the overhang should be no more than 25 per cent of 3 metres (10 feet), which is equal to 75 cm (2 feet, 6 inches). This method is good for covering old paving that needs to be replaced or is unsafe.

CANTILEVER DECKING

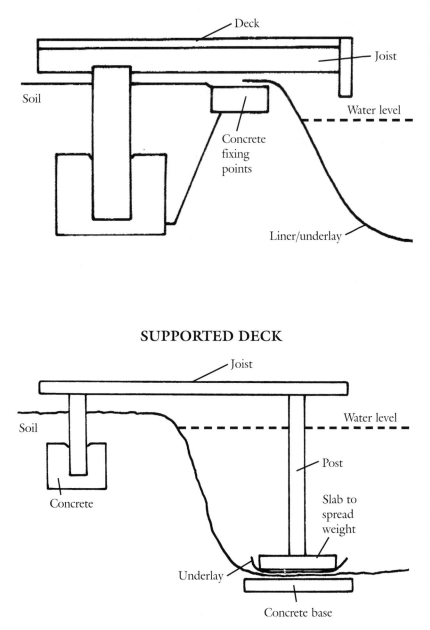

Deck

Joist

Soil

Water level

Concrete
fixing
points

Liner/underlay

SUPPORTED DECK

Joist

Water level

Soil

Post

Concrete

Slab to
spread
weight

Underlay

Concrete base

If you have a very large pond, you can support the decking with posts. When the pond is built, a large paving slab (60 cm x 60 cm, or 2 feet by 2 feet, is ideal) is laid on to the liner on a square of underlay (to protect the liner from damage), and a post can stand on this. As the weight is spread over such a large area, it will not damage the liner. The post will need to be treated to stop it absorbing water. There are wax coatings on better-quality decking that do exactly this.

A FINAL NOTE

The only factor affecting the material used for edging is the size of the budget you have for the project. An important tip to remember is that, once done, it is quite difficult and expensive to change the edge, so think carefully before you install it.

> *Note: In areas of soft soil, such as sand, a concrete base will need to be built under the liner to provide a stable level base on which to stand the post. The post should be sized accordingly.*

CHAPTER 3

BUILDING WATERFALLS AND STREAMS

1. Pre-formed water courses
2. Liner water courses
3. Concrete water courses

When ponds are being planned, the waterfall and stream section is often left out until the last minute. Don't make this mistake because, often, the spoil from the dig can be utilised for the 'fall' of the waterfall, rather than carting it away off site. This is an easy option and can save you money.

WATERFALL CONSTRUCTION

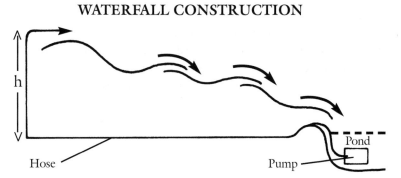

h = 'Head' of water. Pump must raise water to run waterfall.

However, there are a number of issues to consider before taking this approach. If there is not a natural fall across the garden, the sudden arrival of a large pile of soil in the middle of it is going to look a little odd. If the garden has a natural fall, adding to the height with the spoil will not be unreasonable. If the garden is flat, a gentle stream/waterfall combination is going to look more at home.

No matter what the size or length of the stream or waterfall, there are a few very obvious items to keep in mind:

1) Water flows downhill! This may seem ridiculous, but the most common problems with waterfalls are leaks. They are often due to the fact that people expect the water to go where they think it should, not where nature and gravity intended.

2) The more water flow required, the wider or deeper the water course will need to be.

3) If the water course is large, the water will evaporate more quickly in the summer months so a regular top-up will be needed, or, better still, use an auto top-up system.

4) For large waterfalls, a by-pass will be required if you have neighbours, so that the water can be diverted to the pond quietly at night. This is also useful in winter to stop the water flow chilling the pond.

5) Never bury the pipework under the water course as it may need replacing at some point, and it is more susceptible to damage during installation.

6) When digging the pond, remember to keep the topsoil separate, as a rockery covered in subsoil is not going to grow plants very well.

7) If a filter is to be installed at the waterfall's supply point, remember to allow for room to hide it.

8) A formal pond requires a formal water course, and a natural pond requires a natural stream/waterfall.

9) If the stream is to be planted, deeper areas are needed to allow for the root system of marginal plants or a planting basket. Planting areas need to be out of the main water flow, otherwise the soil will be washed away.

10) Compact the newly moved soil well, as it will sink and the water course will move. This can lead to leaks, and, in the case of waterfalls built from concrete, will often break them in half.

PRE-FORMED WATER COURSES

The quickest and simplest way to build a water course is to use a pre-formed one. They are readily available and are supplied finished in various colours, textures and shapes. There are new materials coming on to the market all the time, which look more and more realistic. The newer ones are so good it is impossible to tell the difference between real and imitation until you touch them.

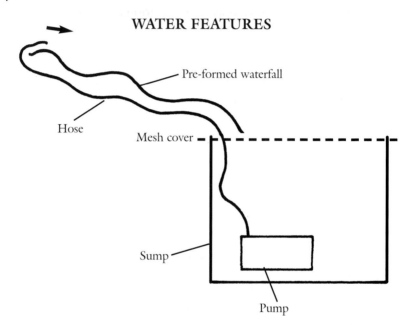

WATER FEATURES

Pre-formed waterfall

Hose

Mesh cover

Sump

Pump

The cheapest material is vacuum-formed plastic. It is very flexible and requires more time and effort to install correctly. The finish is poor and colours are very limited. The other major drawback of plastic is that the smooth surface of the material does not allow the algae to get a good grip and grow on it to help disguise it. The nature of plastic stops the colour from fading and it will not 'blend in' as the pond matures.

Fibre glass was the first material for pre-formed water courses and still offers the best value for money. It is ridged and strong, so it is easy to install and maintain. The colours are almost unlimited and the surface can be covered in real stone chips to give the effect of rock. New lightweight polyurethane foams are becoming more popular as weight can be a problem with some of the larger fibre glass items. The finish is similar to fibre glass and the detail is even better, as the process allows for better moulding techniques. The colours are probably the best and most realistic yet seen.

You can also buy units made from glass fibres and concrete, instead of resin. This gives the unit the perfect finish as it is rock solid. The drawback is weight. Even small units are very heavy and they are fragile, making installation a two-person job.

INSTALLATION

Lay the water course sections out in the order that you would like and mark out a rough outline so that you can see where you are going to excavate. Remove the sections and dig out to the depth required plus 5 cm (2 inches), to allow for the sand underlay. Spread the sand over the area and lay the lowest section first. Make sure the section falls towards the pond. Using a level will be almost impossible, so the best way is to use the garden hose to run water down the water course and adjust the fall until it works without any water overflowing into the wrong areas. Pack sand around the lower section to secure in position. Place the next section in position and again use the hose to check the flow is going in the right direction. Check the overhang into the second section to make sure all the water is going on and not disappearing back under the lip.

Even a drip can empty a pond quicker than you may think. With all the sections in and running, secure them in place, using either a lean mix of sand and cement (five parts sand to one part cement) or compacted soil.

PREVENTING LEAKS

Where pre-formed sections overlap, it is possible to get a leak.

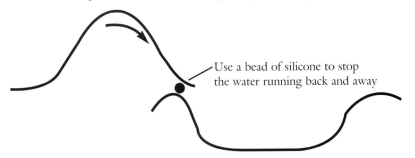

Use a bead of silicone to stop the water running back and away

USING PRE-FORMED SECTIONS

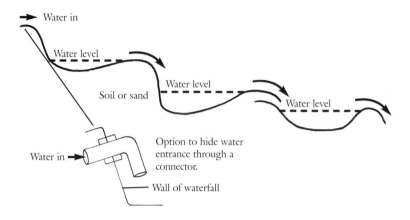

Water in

Water level

Soil or sand

Water level

Water level

Water in

Option to hide water entrance through a connector.

Wall of waterfall

LINER WATER COURSES

As before, dig out the shape of the waterfall and dig down to the depth required for each pool. The floor of the pools should fall away from the pond so that water will stay in each pool when the pump is switched off. The top or header pool needs to be deeper, as you will be pumping the water into this one and the water will need to slow down before it flows over the lip to the next pool.

When the excavation is finished, remove any stones or roots that may be present and compact the soil down to minimise the risk of movement. Cover the area with underlay, wet it down with a hose, and spray to hold it in place. Unroll the liner over the underlay and fit as best you can. Cover the liner with underlay to protect it from damage. Now the rock fitting can take place.

Lay out the rocks so that you can see what shapes and sizes you have. Wash them to remove dust, and you will be able to see the colour they will be when water is flowing over them. Starting at the bottom, lay the rocks in their final place but do not fix them yet. Use a small level to ensure the lip to the next pool is the lowest point in each pool.

Once the whole waterfall is in place, stand back and make sure it all looks as you expect. If any rock looks out of place, remove it and try another. When you are finally satisfied with the arrangement, remove the rocks in reverse order and lay them out on the ground. Mix a good, strong mortar with added waterproofing agent, lay a thick bed in the first pool and place the rocks as you planned. Work your way up to the top pool. Use more mortar than you need, as it is easier to remove excess than add more once all the rocks are in place. Stand back and check again. If you are satisfied with the look, you can go back and fill all the gaps with mortar.

> *Tip: If there are larger gaps than you would like between the rocks, you can embed small pieces of rock in the mortar to help hide them.*

To hide all the liner and underlay, cover all the visible areas with a layer of mortar mixed with sharp sand. This will give a more rock-like finish than plain builders' sand.

The liner on the outside of the water course has to be held up against the rock to stop any water escaping. As the soil is built up along the edge of the waterfall, the liner will be held in position. Any excess liner can be cut off. To prevent leaks, do not let soil touch the water or it will soak away. Once you have planted your rockery, the rock work will blend in and any less-than-perfect areas will be covered.

CONCRETE WATER COURSES

Building a waterfall from concrete is more daunting than building a pond, as the smaller amounts of material used leave the finished structure quite weak and susceptible to cracking.

It is really important that you have a firm base to build from. A pile of recently dug soil will move, and break the back of the long, thin types of constructions that occur with concrete water courses. Concrete is really the choice for larger projects, as it gets stronger the bigger the structure becomes.

The advantages of this building method are:
1) You can use much larger rocks, as there is no liner to damage.
2) There is no restriction on the waterfall's height.

Concrete tips:
- *Concrete is a mix of cement and ballast (sand and stones).*
- *For water courses, a mix of four parts ballast to one part cement will be strong enough.*

- *Use a mixer for the best results. Hand-mixing can give poor consistency and result in leaks and structural failure.*
- *Always use a good waterproofing agent. Read the instructions, as too much may weaken the concrete.*
- *Don't build in frosty weather. If you must, be sure to cover up the work to stop it freezing or you will have to do it all over again.*
- *Don't mix concrete antifreeze and waterproofers.*
- *Wear gloves and eye protection when mixing or handling cement products. They can burn skin.*
- *If your fish are near the work area, cover them to prevent cement dust entering the water, or it will kill them.*
- *Cover the work up when you have finished and allow it to dry **slowly**. The longer the concrete takes to dry, the stronger it will be.*
- *In hot weather, spray water over the concrete to slow down the drying process.*

CONCRETE WATER COURSE

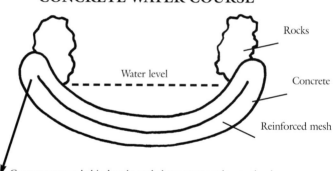

Concrete comes behind rocks and above proposed water level.

When you have decided on the shape of your feature, excavate the depth required plus the depth of the concrete. For small features, a thickness of 10 cm (4 inches) should suffice, but, as the feature grows, so will the amount of concrete that is needed. If the rocks are very large, you may need foundations.

Lay a waterproof membrane over the excavation to stop the ground soaking the water from the concrete and drying it too

Tip: It is now possible to add reinforcing fibres (in the form of glass fibre) to the concrete mix to give added strength to the structure. But this is not a replacement for reinforcing mesh.

fast. Lay about half of the thickness of concrete to be used and then push in a reinforcing mesh and cover it with the rest of the concrete. Place any rocks that are to be used and push them well into the concrete making sure they are securely fixed in place.

The rocks should sit on the reinforcing mesh as they will place an extra load on the concrete due to their weight. The concrete has to come up behind the rocks to ensure that the water course is watertight. This is important as some rocks, such as sandstone, will allow water to pass through them. With taller, larger waterfalls, foundations will be required to hold the weight of the rocks. A simple feature such as the one shown below can be built on an extended section of the pond's collar.

The lower splash pool is necessary to stop the waterfall disturbing the entire pond surface and making it impossible to see the fish. The first step is to build the lower pool. Allow the concrete to harden before carrying on with the next section, but try not to let it cure as the joint will be more difficult to waterproof. As the rock wall is built, the concrete can be added behind it. Use a dryish mix so that it does not run out of the gaps between the rocks or push the wall over. Remember to embed the reinforcing as you go. It should be covered totally in concrete, otherwise it will rust.

EXTENDED COLLAR

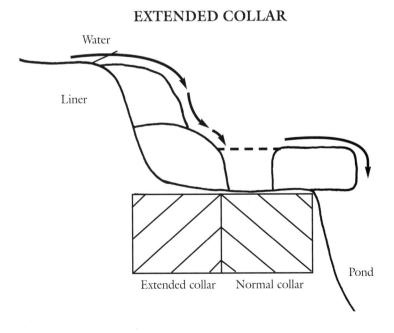

Water

Liner

Extended collar   Normal collar

Pond

WATERFALL FOUNDATIONS

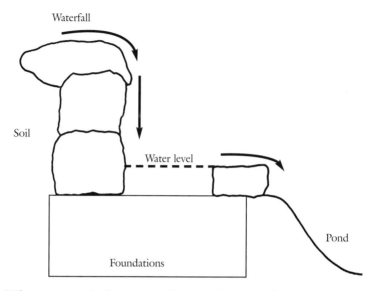

When you reach the top section, lay the rest of the concrete and reinforcing mesh. As before, place the rocks into concrete and push in firmly. Back up the concrete behind to waterproof the feature, and finally secure the rocks. The whole structure should be left to dry. It can then be washed down and painted with a lime neutraliser.

> *Note: If there are already fish in the pond, do not let the washdown water flow in as it could kill the fish.*

LONG WATER COURSES

Building long streams can cause problems when using concrete, as the thickness of the materials used is not sufficient to hold the weight should the soil move. A simple way to get over this is to build the feature in sections, although providing a flexible joint between them can be difficult, and often the joints are not watertight. You need to ensure that the higher section overlaps the lower, so that water flows down into the lower water course.

This method is very difficult, so the use of a liner underneath the concrete is the best way to ensure that the water course stays watertight. Even if small leaks occur, the water will find its way back to the pond.

CHAPTER 4

PLANTING THE POND

1. Marginal plants
2. Submerged and oxygenating plants
3. Water lilies
4. Floating plants
5. Bog plants

Before planting your pond, you need to consider the environment that you have created and the prevailing conditions – is it a shady site, or is it open and windy? The most important aspect of the water plants is their effect on the pond's water quality. In most natural ponds, there is a generous surface covering of aquatic plants, such as water lilies or water hawthorn and even floating plants such as frog bit or duck weed.

Unless you plan to specialise in koi, which will eat or disturb your plants, you should concentrate on providing plenty of submerged and floating leaf plants to start with. These will help to control the green algae that will try to take over the pond.

To maintain a healthy balance in the garden pond you need a high ratio of plants to fish. The waste produced by the fish will encourage microscopic algae (green water) to reproduce in vast numbers, and, if the ornamental plants cannot absorb the mineral by-products quickly enough, submerged plants may be killed off by the lack of light.

After the hard landscaping of the pond, the plants provide the finishing touch, so before you go shopping for them, spend some time researching the right combination. For example, do not choose a selection of plants that are all in flower at the same time, otherwise the pond will be colourless for the rest of the season. You need to select plants that will give flowers and foliage for as many months as possible.

In the first year, the plants may not give enough coverage so you will have to add some extra floating plants or oxygenators to keep the water balance right. Mixed baskets of water plants are often seen for sale. These are very pretty for the first year, then the strongest plants take over and the others die off, so they are best avoided. Remember, it will be two to three years before most of the plants are at their best, so be patient.

While every effort has been made to provide accurate plant names, readers should note that taxonomy is reviewed every year and names are subject to change. Some plants may not be available under the same names given here.

MARGINAL PLANTS

Marginals are so called for the obvious reason that they like to grow around the edge of the pond, in the margins where the water is quite shallow. In the wild, they are very useful for supporting the bank and surrounding area to prevent soil erosion. In a garden pond, they are not required for this function, but they have other attributes that improve the look and quality of the habitat. They soften the hard edge of the pond surround, offer shade to pond wildlife, and a home for smaller inhabitants.

Marginals bring colour to the pond by flowering when submerged plants are still dormant, and, if cut back, often go on flowering right through the season. In simple terms they are the herbaceous border of the pond.

TIPS ON PURCHASING MARGINALS
• *Do not buy plants in the autumn (fall) after they have died down. Wait until spring, when fresh growth can be seen.*
• *Do not buy a selection of plants that are all in flower at once. This will make for a dull pond for the rest of the year.*

- *Often, seedlings are offered for sale. However, unless they are a true species (i.e. not a man-made hybrid), they will not be true to flower colour, height or habitat. Therefore, unless you have a large, natural pond to plant, they are best avoided.*
- *Make sure there is a label on each plant, otherwise you will not know what you have got when you get home.*
- *Check to see that plants are in pond baskets and the correct soil. If not, remember to purchase the right baskets and soil for the plants.*
- *Check all plants to make sure they are hardy enough for your pond. Some plants may not tolerate windy conditions but will be fine in a shady position.*

Acorus calamus
Common name: Sweet Flag.
Conditions: Wet, humus-rich soil to 15 cm (6 inches).
Position: Sun or full shade.
Propagation: Seeds rarely ripen in colder climates. Rhizome division is the best method.
Description: The sweet flag is a marsh and shallow-water plant that grows from a creeping rhizome. It is very hardy and almost an evergreen in all but the coldest winters. It produces yellow flowers 7 to 10 cm (2.75 to 4 inches) long in late spring and early summer. It grows to a height of 120 cm (4 feet). The rhizome was once used in confectionery manufacturing.

OTHER VARIETIES
Acorus gramineus ogon: This is a very good variety, although it can be difficult to obtain, with bright, golden leaves. It is best grown in a sunny position to keep the golden colour.
Acorus gramineus 'Variegatus': This smaller species grows up to 30 cm (1 foot). It is ideal for small ponds or for growing in pots.
Acorus 'Variegatus': Probably the best-known form of this plant. It has striking green-and-yellow/white variegation that is pink-tinged as it starts to grow. It may reach 1 m (3 feet, 3 inches) tall.

Alisma plantago
Common name: Water Plantain.
Conditions: Grows best in rich, muddy, slightly acid soil.
Position: Full sun to full shade.

Propagation: Seed or root division in spring.
Description: The water plantain grows a rosette of large, spoon-shaped leaves with well-defined veins running their length. Throughout the summer, a pyramid of white, sometimes pink-tinted, flowers can be seen on a stem rising 60 cm (2 feet) from the centre of the leaves. It is best to remove the spent flowers before they set seed, as the plant can spread quite quickly across any damp ground.

OTHER VARIETIES
Alisma parviflora: Similar to *A. plantago,* but has broader, rounder leaves.
Alisma lanceolatum: Has thinner, upright leaves tapering at the end.

Butomus umbellatus
Common name: Flowering Rush.
Conditions: Thrives in rich, slightly acid, peaty soil.
Position: Full sun or half shade.
Propagation: Rhizome division in spring.
Description: The flowering rush has rich green leaves that are triangular in section and can reach 90 cm (3 ft) in height. The clusters of pink flowers in late summer are even taller, although it can be some time before the plant is mature enough to flower. It will grow in up to 25 cm (10 inches) of water, but it does best in more shallow water, up to 5 cm (2 inches) over the soil.

Caltha palustris
Common name: Marsh Marigold.
Conditions: Does best in rich, muddy, slightly acid soil.
Position: Sun to semi-shade.
Propagation: Seed, or root division in spring.
Description: The marsh marigold or kingcup really is a must for the pond. It is the first to flower in the spring and one of the most prolific growers. It can be planted to depths of 20 cm (8 inches) over the crown. It forms a mound of glossy green leaves on stems up to 45 cm (18 inches) long, with yellow, buttercup flowers held above. It needs cutting down in mid-summer to encourage new growth, as old leaves can develop mildew and look untidy.

OTHER VARIETIES
Caltha palustris alba: A compact, white-flowered variety, which
grows to a height of 20 to 30 cm (8 to 10 inches).
Caltha palustris 'Flore Plena': A small, double-yellow-flowered
variety. It is ideal for a small pond as it does not multiply
quickly. Grows to a height of 10 to 20 cm (4 to 8 inches). It
requires a water depth of no more than 5 to 10 cm (2 to 4
inches) over the crown – the shallower the better.
Caltha palustris l. var polypetela: A vigorous species suited to the
largest ponds only. Grows to a height of 80 to 100 cm (2 feet,
4 inches to 3 feet, 6 inches) in a water depth of 35 cm (14
inches).

Carex elata 'Bowles Golden'
Common name: Golden Sedge.
Conditions: Does best in rich, muddy, slightly acid soil.
Position: Full sun to full shade.
Propagation: Division in spring. It can be grown from seed, but
often not true to type.
Description: The golden sedge is not really a water plant but it
adapts readily to the pond environment, although it does best
in a bog. An excellent plant for the darker corner of the pond,
it will stay golden even in the shade. 'Bowles Golden' creates a
mound of golden leaves with black flowers held above it in late
summer.

Cotula coronopifolia
Common name: Golden Buttons.
Conditions: Damp, to 10 cm (4 inches) water depth.
Position: Sun or semi-shade.
Propagation: Cuttings or seed in early summer.
Description: A good, low-growing marginal, up to 10 cm (4
inches), which offers colour from early spring to late autumn.
Thin, bright-green leaves offer a fresh background to the yellow
flowers that have no petals surrounding them.

Equisetum hyemale
Common name: Dutch or Scouring Rush.
Conditions: Any moist soil to 15 cm (6 inches) depth.

Position: Sun or semi-shade.
Propagation: Division of stolons in late summer.
Description: Often called horsetail rushes, these plants form compact clumps of tall, leafless stems with black rings segmenting the length. Mixed with other plants, they provide a contrasting form. Can grow to 1.5 metres (5 feet) in ideal conditions.

OTHER VARIETIES
Equisetum scripoides: The arctic version, which grows to 25 cm (10 inches) tall and has fine, dark-green solid stems. Good for smaller ponds and water features.

Eriophorum angustifolium
Common name: Cotton Grass.
Conditions: Wet soil, preferably acidic, 2 cm (just under an inch) of water.
Position: Any.
Propagation: Division or seed.
Description: Marsh grass with white, tufted seed heads that look like cotton wool (cotton), hence its common name. It grows to about 40 cm (16 inches). It is ideal for smaller ponds. It is a very hardy plant that can withstand windy, exposed areas.

Glyceria maxima variegata
Common name: Gardener's Garters.
Conditions: Does best in rich, muddy soil.
Position: Full sun to full shade.
Propagation: Division in spring.
Description: A striking plant with beautiful green and creamy-white striped leaves that are flushed pink when young. Like most grasses it can be invasive, but planted in a basket it can be controlled. Not suitable for a clay-bottomed pond.

Hippuris vulgaris
Common name: Mare's Tail.
Conditions: Does best in humus-rich soil.
Position: Sunny.
Propagation: Rhizome division.

Description: Forms large clumps of fine green foliage above the water and can even grow totally submerged to a depth of several metres. Needs regular attention to prevent it from taking over the pond, and it should be grown in a container to aid management. Maximum height above the water can be 80 cm (2 feet, 9 inches) or more.

Houttuynia cordata 'Chamaeleon'
Conditions: Does best in any moist soil, except chalk.
Position: Full sun to full shade.
Propagation: Seed or root division in spring.
Description: A most unusual plant in that the leaves are red, green, yellow and white in no particular order or combination. The same plant will vary its colours from season to season and from year to year. It will grow in any soil, from wet to dry, so it can be invasive if not controlled. It also produces small, white flowers in late summer.

OTHER VARIETIES
Houttuynia cordata: The common form, with green, heart-shaped leaves and red stems. Small flowers are held above the foliage in mid-summer, surrounded by four white bracts.
Houttuynia cordata 'Flore Plena': As *H. cordata,* but a double row of bracts around the flower.

Iris pseudacorus
Common name: Yellow Flag Iris.
Conditions: Any moist soil.
Position: Full sun to full shade.
Propagation: Seed or rhizome division in spring.
Description: The flag iris is a strong grower with a free-flowering nature and large yellow flowers. The dark green foliage, up to 100 cm (3 feet, 3 inches) tall creates an imposing plant in all but the smallest pond. Confine to a basket for best results and to control the root system.

OTHER VARIETIES
Iris p. bastardii: A selected form with pale yellow flowers.
Iris p. 'Flore Pleno': This variety has double flowers.

Iris p. 'Variegata': Slower growing, this very good, yellow-green variegated variety also flowers in early summer. Variegation fades to green in late summer.

Iris laevigata
Conditions: Does best in any moist acid soil.
Position: Full sun to full shade.
Propagation: Seed or rhizome division in spring.
Description: A very hardy iris with strong, glossy green leaves up to 80 cm (2 feet, 6 inches) tall. Clear blue flowers are readily produced even in young plants. Will grow in water up to 15 cm (6 inches) deep over the rhizome.

OTHER VARIETIES
Iris l. 'Colchesterensis': A strong cultivar with flowers blotched with white and mauve.
Iris l. 'Midnight': Dark blue, clematis-like flower with a white throat.
Iris l. 'Snowdrift': As *I. laevigata,* but has large, white flowers with a pale mauve throat.
Iris l. 'Variegata': Clear blue flowers with cream-green variegated leaves. Slower growing, but one of the best variegated plants of the pond.

Iris versicolor
Common name: Blue Flag Iris.
Conditions: Does best in any moist soil, except chalk.
Position: Full sun to full shade.
Propagation: Seed or rhizome division in spring.
Description: The American blue flag is an ideal iris for the smaller pond because of its restrained growth, although it reaches 60 cm (3 feet) in height. Narrow, bright green leaves make for a compact plant. The violet-blue flowers are held on stems 45 cm (18 inches) high. It does best in shallow water 2 to 4 cm (1 to 1.5 inches) above the roots.

OTHER VARIETIES
Iris v. 'Gerald Darby': This has very decorative foliage, purple at the base, changing to green. It has large, purple-violet flowers

with a white throat and bright yellow veins.

Iris v. 'Kermesina': Well-formed, violet-purple flowers with a golden yellow and white veining on the throat.

Iris v. lavender: This has lavender flowers, but may be difficult to obtain.

Iris v. vernal: A purple-to-pink flower with a white throat. Ideal for smaller ponds as it grows to 50 cm (20 inches) only. May be registered under a different name, and difficult to obtain.

Juncus effusus spiralis
Common name: Spiral Rush.
Conditions: Does best in any moist soil.
Position: Sun to semi-shade.
Propagation: Seed or division of crowns in late spring.
Description: A strange plant, its spirals of green cylindrical leaves go in all directions, unlike the straight spikes of its relatives.

OTHER VARIETIES
Juncus effusus: Green-gold leaves, with brown clusters of seed heads. It grows to about 50 cm (20 inches).
Juncus ensifolius: The soft rush grows to a height of 80 cm (30 inches) and in a water depth of 10 cm (4 inches). Best planted in a container as it can be invasive. Flowers are brown balls on the tips of the stems all year round.

Lobelia cardinalis
Conditions: Does best in any moist soil.
Position: Full sun and semi-shade.
Propagation: Seed or division in late spring.
Description: A very striking plant even before it flowers. The dark-red stems and foliage are immediately visible around any pond. It is a herbaceous plant, but does well in water away from its arch-enemy, the slug. The flowers are a strong crimson on long, thin stems up to 1 metre (40 inches) tall. They open a few at a time, so the flowers seem to last for months.

OTHER VARIETIES
Lobelia 'Cinnabar Rose': Similar to *L. cardinalis*, but with branching, salmon-pink flowers over green leaves.

Lobelia 'Dark Crusader': Purplish-green leaves with dark-red flowers. Grows up to 120 cm (4 feet).
Lobelia 'Fan Orchidrosa': Rich-pink flowers and fresh green leaves, previously known as *Lobelia 'Orchard Rose'.*
Lobelia 'Queen Victoria': A cultivar with shiny purple leaves followed by deep, cardinal-red flowers.
Lobelia vedrariensis: This plant has deep-blue flowers over lush green foliage.

Lobelia syphilitica
Conditions: Does best in any moist soil.
Position: Sun to semi-shade.
Propagation: Seed or division in spring.
Description: This variety can grow up to 90 cm (3 feet) tall with blue-violet flowers on stems of green foliage. The flowers are relatively short-lived.

OTHER VARIETIES
Lobelia s. 'Alba': A white-flowered variety. Grows up to 180 cm (6 feet) high.

Lysichiton americanus
Common name: Skunk Cabbage.
Conditions: Prefers deep, rich peaty soil, but grows well in heavy soil. Grow on the margin to 10 cm (4 inches) of water depth.
Position: Full sun to get the best, but can tolerate some shade.
Propagation: Fresh seed in late summer.
Description: The skunk cabbage is one of the most magnificent water plants. In spring, large bright-yellow spathes are produced, followed by wide, mid-green leaves up to 1 metre (40 inches) tall.

OTHER VARIETIES
Lysichiton camtschatcensis: Similar to *L. americanus* but with white spathes and a height of 75cm (2 feet, 6 inches).

Lysimachia nummularia
Common name: Creeping Jenny.
Conditions: Does best in any moist soil.

Position: Sun to semi-shade.
Propagation: Cuttings any time of the year.
Description: One of my favourite plants, this will grow anywhere and over anything. Bright green leaves covered in butter yellow flowers. A very versatile plant for the pond and surrounding area.

OTHER VARIETIES
Lysimachia n. 'Aurea': Its yellow-golden leaves are burnt by direct sun, so it is best planted in the shade.
Lysimachia punctata: This plant has tall, erect stems reaching 20 cm (8 inches) in height, with clusters of small, primrose-yellow flowers.
Lysimachia thyrsiflora: Bears no resemblance to *L. nummularia*. A tall-growing species with pale green, spear-shaped leaves. Flowers are densely packed in a pyramid cluster. It can grow to 80 cm (32 inches) in shallow water, up to 5 cm (2 inches) over the roots. Propagate by division of the main plant after flowering.

Lythrum salicaria
Common name: Purple Loosestrife.
Conditions: Does best in any moist soil.
Position: Sun to semi-shade.
Propagation: Division of main plant or from seed.
Description: Thin green leaves are held below tall spikes of pink flowers that bloom from mid-summer to early autumn. There are a number of varieties, ranging from 45 cm to 1.5 metres (18 inches to 4 feet, 6 inches) tall, so there is a type to suit all tastes and pond sizes.

OTHER VARIETIES
Lythrum s. augenweide: Reddish-violet flowers up to 1 metre (40 inches) tall.
Lythrum s. 'Robert': Clear pink flowers held about 75 to 90 cm (2 feet, 6 inches to 3 feet) above ground. Ideal for most ponds.
Lythrum virgatum: This plant is ideal for smaller ponds as it grows to 60 cm (2 feet) only. It has red flowers, which grow in long narrow spikes.

Mentha aquatica
Common name: Aquatic Mint.
Conditions: Does best in any moist soil.
Position: Sun to full shade.
Propagation: Root cuttings in late spring or from seed.
Description: The water mint is a very fast-growing plant that can soon take over the pond. But its attraction is the small, oval aromatic leaves and purple 'balls' of flowers that bring so many insects during the summer. Cut back after flowering and it soon repays you with more flowers and foliage. Grows to 90 cm (3 ft).

OTHER VARIETIES
Mentha cervina: A native of the Mediterranean region, it has thin green leaves with a most pungent peppermint scent when crushed. The lilac flowers are also strongly perfumed. Height to 30 cm (1 foot).
Mentha cervina alba: As above, but a white-flowered cultivar.
Mentha crispa: Bright green, curled leaves to a height of 45 cm (18 inches).
Mentha pulegium: Known as the Penny Royal.
Mentha rubra: As above but with red-to-violet leaves. Grows up to 60 cm (2 feet) tall.

Menyanthes trifoliata
Common name: Bog Bean.
Conditions: Very wet to 30 cm (1 foot) of water over plant.
Position: Sun or semi-shade.
Propagation: From seed or rhizome division in spring.
Description: The bog bean is an attractive plant that holds three lobbed leaves on stakes above the creeping stems. In early summer, a cluster of white flowers rises above the foliage, and often again in the autumn (fall). It prefers peaty acid soil for best results. Height to 30 cm (1 foot) above the water surface.

Mimulus luteus
Common name: Monkey Flower.
Conditions: Any moist soil.
Position: Sun or shade.
Propagation: Seed or cuttings any time of year.

Description: The monkey musk is one of the earliest plants to flower, and, if dead-headed, it can bloom all summer and into the autumn (fall). If you allow it to set seed, it soon appears everywhere.

OTHER VARIETIES
Mimulus guttatus: Large yellow flowers with dark red spots over mid-green leaves. Brightens even the darkest corner.
Mimulus 'Lothian Fire': A rare plant with larger, flame-coloured flowers. It tolerates moving water.
Mimulus ringens: Delicate stems with delicate, lilac-coloured flowers. Grows to approximately 40 cm (16 inches).
Other varieties are available but most are not winter hardy.

Myosotis scorpioides
Common name: Water Forget-Me-Not.
Conditions: Moist to 20 cm (8 inches) water depth.
Position: Sun or semi-shade.
Propagation: Seed or cuttings in early spring
Description: The water forget-me-not, with its small, pale-blue flowers held so close to the water surface, is familiar to most people. A rather straggly grower, but, if trimmed, it forms a good mat in the margins.

OTHER VARIETIES
Mysosotis s. alba: A smaller-growing variety that has white flowers and smaller, lighter-green leaves. More difficult to obtain than *Myositis scorpioides.*
Mysosotis s. 'Mermaid': An improved hybrid that is even more free-flowering and has larger green leaves.

Myriophyllum aquaticum
Common name: Parrot's Feather.
Conditions: Must be grown in water.
Position: Full sun or dappled shade.
Propagation: Offsets root easily.
Description: Bright green, feathery foliage that floats on the water surface. Care needs to be taken as it can be invasive. Will not tolerate prolonged freezing.

Nasturtian officinale
Common name: Water Cress.
Conditions: Best grown in a basket filled with gravel, to
encourage the plant to use waterborne nutrients to combat
algae.
Position: Sun or shade. Will grow anywhere.
Propagation: Cuttings or seed in spring to late autumn (fall).
Description: Water cress, one of the fastest-growing pond plants,
is excellent for helping to control green water and blanket
weed. Fresh green leaves appear all through the season as it
advances around the pond. It needs regular cutting back to
encourage more compact growth. Once it has flowered, the
seed heads need to be removed as soon as possible, otherwise
the plant dies back.

Oenanthe javanica 'Flamingo'
Conditions: Any moist soil to 15 cm (6 inches) of water depth.
Position: Sunny, to get the best variegation.
Propagation: Root cuttings in spring.
Description: A creeping plant that sends up variegated shoots of
green, white and pink that branch out into leafy stems. The
pink fades as the leaves age. Grown for its foliage, it needs to
be contained as it can be invasive.

Petasites hybridus
Common name: Butter Burr.
Conditions: Rich, heavy soil in a container to prevent spreading.
Position: Sun or shade.
Propagation: Division of roots in spring or autumn (fall).
Description: A fast-growing, sometimes invasive, spreading
plant. In late spring, clusters of pale pink flowers are followed
by large, mid-green, heart-shaped leaves. The plant reaches a
height up to 40 cm (16 inches) in a water depth of 10 cm (4
inches).

OTHER VARIETIES
There are several other varieties of this plant, all of which are
best grown in moist, well-drained soil. Generally, damp soil is
preferred to a bog environment.

Phalaris arundinacea picta
Common name: Canary Grass or Ribbon Grass.
Conditions: Dry soil to submerged in 30 cm (1 foot) of water.
Position: Sunny.
Propagation: Seeds and division of crowns.
Description: A graceful grass with an invasive habit, so is best grown in a flower pot to stop it spreading across the pond and garden. Cut down each spring to encourage the younger growth, which has a more vivid colour.

OTHER VARIETIES
Phalaris arundinacea: The common form, often seen near rivers and wetlands, can grow up to 2 metres (6 feet), so it is not suited to smaller ponds. It can be grown in large pots to great effect.

Pontederia cordata
Common name: Pickerel Weed.
Conditions: Heavy, rich, neutral to acid soil. In water up to 40 cm (16 inches) deep.
Position: Sun or semi-shade.
Propagation: Divide root ball in early summer.
Description: Pontederia cordata is one of the most undersold of all pond plants. It has large, glossy and striking leaves, which are green and spear-shaped and which set off the dark-blue flower spikes that are held above them in late summer. It can grow up to 65 cm (26 inches) high.

OTHER VARIETIES
Pontederia cordata alba: Not quite as tall, but has white flowers held above lighter-green leaves.
Pontederia cordata lancifiola: A taller-growing species, to 1 metre (40 inches), which has narrower leaves.

Ranunculus lingua
Common name: Water Buttercup.
Conditions: Damp soil to 80 cm (32 inches) water depth.
Position: Sun or shade.
Propagation: Seed or division of plants in spring.

Description: The water buttercup is suitable for larger ponds only, as it can grow to 1.2 metres (4 feet). The long, spear-shaped leaves and large yellow flowers, seen from spring to autumn, will grace any pond. For the smaller pond, go for *R. flammula*, with its small yellow flowers held in a bunch 45 cm (18 inches) high. It is unusual, as it grows in all but the coldest winters, offering greenery when most other plants have died down.

OTHER VARIETIES
Ranunculus flammula: Commonly known as lesser spearwort, this is one of the few plants to grow during the winter months. It can grow to 30 cm (1 foot) tall and its bright yellow flowers are produced from May to September. To stop it spreading, remove old flower heads before it can set seed. Excellent for smaller ponds. Plant in damp soil or up to 20 cm (8 inches) of water.
Ranunculus fluitans: Not often seen for sale, it has small white flowers and bundles of drooping leaves. It prefers streams and rivers to ponds, and will grow in 1 metre (40 inches) of water. It provides ideal shelter for aquatic life.
Ranunculus lingua 'Grandiflora': Long, deep-green leaves with large, buttercup-coloured flowers.

Sagittaria sagittifolia 'Flore Pleno'
Common name: Arrowhead Plant.
Conditions: Heavy soil with one-third rich humus, in water up to 40 cm (16 inches) deep.
Position: Sun or semi-shade.
Propagation: Seed (not double-flowered variety) or stolons.
Description: The aptly named arrowhead, has arrow-shaped leaves that are a glossy mid-green. These offset the triangular stems of double-white flowers, grouped in threes at intervals along it.

It requires a rich, acid soil and shallow water to achieve its full potential. The plant produces bulb-like stolons at the end of the season and these are used for propagation.

OTHER VARIETIES
Sagittaria sagittifolia: This has single flowers with a purple eye.

Saururus cernuus
Common name: Lizard Tail.
Conditions: Damp soil or water to 45 cm (18 inches) deep.
Position: Sun, semi-shade.
Propagation: Root division.
Description: The lizard tail plant has a long 'tail' of tiny, white fragrant flowers in mid-summer and olive-green, heart-shaped leaves that are brighter on the underside. *Saururus cernuus* is a good plant for the pond, as it is one of the few marginals to have autumn colour, the leaves turning a bright crimson. This plant can grow up to 120 cm (4 feet) in sheltered conditions.

Schoenoplectus lacustris tabernaemontani 'Albescens'
Common name: Stripped Rush.
Conditions: Damp acid soil to 30 cm (1 foot) deep.
Position: Sun or shade.
Propagation: Crown division in spring.
Description: An elegant, tall, green-and-white vertically-striped rush that produces a dense growth in a few seasons. Needs to be repotted or fed every year to avoid thin, short growth. Cut back in winter, to about 15 cm (6 inches), and re-trim in spring to remove older growth and encourage new. Grows to a height of 120 cm (4 feet).

OTHER VARIETIES
Schoenoplectus lacustris tabernaemontani: The green rush grows to 2 metres (6 feet, 6 inches) tall.
Schoenoplectus lacustris zebrinus: As above, but with horizontally-striped leaves.
Scirpus cernuus: This is a delicate grass. Each blade is tipped with a tiny, silver seed head. It grows to a height of 15 cm (6 inches).

Scrophularia aquatica
Common name: Limelight Plant.
Conditions: Any soil in water up to 20 cm (8 inches).
Position: Sunny to keep variegation.
Propagation: Cuttings in spring or crown division.

Description: A very bright foliage plant with oval, green-and-cream/yellow leaves. Small red flowers are often produced, but are best removed to encourage fresh leaf growth. Can grow and spread to 1 metre by 1 metre (3 feet by 3 feet), so it is best to trim back old growth to keep a compact shape. In turn, this will encourage new growth.

Sisyrinchium californicum
Conditions: Moist to wet soil.
Position: Full sun or dappled shade.
Propagation: Seeds readily, so can be invasive.
Description: Iris-type leaves with star-shaped, yellow flowers. Grows to 20 cm (8 inches).

Syn cyperus involucratus
Common name: Umbrella Grass or Umbrella Palm.
Conditions: Does best in rich, heavy soil, such as clay.
Position: Hot and sunny.
Propagation: Seed or root division in early summer.
Description: The umbrella palm, an architectural plant for the pond, has a thin, green stem up to 60 cm (2 feet) tall, which supports a star-shaped formation of lime-green foliage with rather insignificant brown flowers. It seeds itself in or out of the pond and spreads quickly. It can be tender in very cold climates, so drop to deeper water for the winter to protect it from frost.

OTHER SPECIES
Cyperus eragrostis: Pale green leaves up to 10 mm (4 inches) wide and 90 to 120 cm (3 to 4 feet) tall. Can be invasive if not kept in check.
Cyperus involucratus: Tall umbrella grass, growing up to 50 cm (20 inches).
Cyperus longus: The sweet galingale, a truly graceful plant with three-sided leafy stems that bear long, reddish-brown flowers. Best left to larger ponds as it grows to 120 cm (4 feet), although it can look striking in the smaller pond if grown in a basket.

RED WATER LILIES

Nymphaea 'Atropurpurea'

Nymphaea 'Charles de Meurville'

Nymphaea 'Froebelii'

Nymphaea 'James Brydon'

Nymphaea 'Lucida'

Nymphaea 'Newton'

Nymphaea 'René Gérard'

Nymphaea 'Splendida'

WHITE WATER LILIES

Nymphaea 'Hermine'

Nymphaea 'Marliacea Albida'

Nymphaea 'Maxima'

Nymphaea odorata minor alba

YELLOW WATER LILIES

Nymphaea 'Joey Tomocik'

Nymphaea 'Marliacea Chromatella'

Nymphaea 'Moorei'

Nymphaea 'Pygmaea Helvola'

PINK WATER LILIES

Nymphaea 'Amabilis'

Nymphaea 'American Star'

Nymphaea 'Fabiola Mrs Richmond'

Nymphaea 'Rossennymphe'

Nymphaea 'Madame Wilfron Gonnère'

Nymphaea 'Masaniello'

Nymphaea 'Pink Sensation'

Nymphaea odorata 'Rose Arey'

UNUSUAL WATER LILIES

Nymphaea 'Comanche'

Nymphaea 'Sioux'

MARGINALS

Acorus
'Variegatus'

Caltha
palustris
(Marsh
Marigold)

Varieties of
Syn cyperus
involucratus
(Umbrella
Grass)
left and right

MARGINALS

Equisetum hyemale (Dutch or Scouring Rush)

Equisetum scripoides (arctic variety of Dutch Rush)

Eriophorum angustifolium (Cotton Grass)

Hippuris vulgarus (Mare's Tail)

Houttuynia cordata

Iris laevigata

Iris pseudacorus (Yellow Flag Iris)

Juncus effusus

MARGINALS

Lobelia
cardinalis

Myrio-
phyllum
aquaticum
(Parrot's
Feather)

Lysimachia
punctata

Lythrum
salicaria
(Purple
Loosestrife)

Mentha
aquatica
(Aquatic
Mint)

Mimulus
luteus
(Monkey
Flower)

Mimulus
'Lothian Fire'

Mimulus
ringens

MARGINALS

Myosotis scorpioides (Water Forget-Me-Not)

Ranunculus lingua 'Grandiflora'

Scirpus cernuus

Schoeno-plectus lacustris zebrinus

Sisyrin-chium californicum

Thalia dealbata (Hardy Canna)

Typha latifolia

SUB-TROPICAL MARGINALS

Canna
longwood
'Ra'

Canna
longwood
'Erebus'

SUBMERGED AND OXYGENATING PLANTS

Aponogeton
distachyos
(Water
Hawthorn)

Orontium
aquaticum
(Golden
Club)

FLOATING PLANTS

Rorippa
nasturtium
aquaticum
('True' Water
Cress)

Stratiotes
aloides
(Water
Soldier)

Thalia dealbata
Common name: Hardy Canna.
Conditions: In water, up to a depth of 25 to 50 cm (10 to 20 inches) over crown.
Position: Full sun.
Propagation: Division or seed.
Description: Tall, sculptured leaves with spears of blue flowers. Grows to a height of 2 metres (6.5 feet) each season and dies back in water.

Typha latifolia 'Variegata'
Common name: Bull Rush.
Conditions: Heavy soil to aid support and a water depth up to 50 cm (20 inches).
Position: Sun for best colour.
Propagation: Root division.
Description: This is the only other reed mace to consider, as the more common ones are far too invasive and grow too large for most ponds. This particular variety grows large too, but not as quickly. However, it is suitable for the larger pond only. The beautiful, pale yellow variegation is very attractive, and, when 1.2 to 1.5 metres (44 to 54 inches) tall, it makes a vivid display.

OTHER VARIETIES
Typha latifolia: Long, grassy leaves with large, brown seed heads. Grows to a height of 120 cm (4 feet).
Typha laxmannii: This has lighter-green/yellow foliage and a globe-shaped flower head to 5 cm (2 inches) in diameter. It grows in deep water and to a height of 120 cm (4 feet).

Typha minima
Common name: Dwarf Bull Rush.
Conditions: Moist soil to 10 cm (4 inches) water depth.
Position: Sun or shade.
Propagation: Crown division or seed.
Description: Ideal for the small pond as its thin, round leaves of dark green are a good contrast to other marginals. It will grow in the most exposed areas without any shelter, but needs to be contained in a pot, as its hardiness means it will outgrow

weaker plants. In autumn (fall), the small, almost round, brown seed heads are formed, and, if left, they soon seed. They make good dried flowers if picked before fully mature.

Veronica beccabunga
Common name: Brook Lime.
Conditions: Wet soil to 20 cm (8 inches) depth.
Position: Sun or semi-shade.
Propagation: Cuttings or seed in spring.
Description: A low creeper that is ideal for the pond edge. It grows to 10 cm (4 inches) tall, has rich, dark-green, oval leaves, and small, blue, forget-me-not-like flowers. It will grow in fast-flowing water, so it is perfect for waterfall or stream areas.

Zantedeschia aethiopica
Common name: Arum Lily.
Conditions: Good, heavy soil with plenty of food, in up to 30 cm (1 foot) of water.
Position: Full sun or semi-shade.
Propagation: Late summer division of rhizome or suckers.
Description: The arum lily is one of the most recognisable of plants, and one of the easiest to grow. In good soil and shallow water for the growing season, it displays dark-green, horn-shaped leaves, and, in late spring or early summer, the whitest flowers (actually spathes) with a bright yellow spadix in the centre. In winter, submerge under 25 cm (9 inches) of water, to protect it from all but the coldest climates, but remember to raise it to shallower water in spring.

OTHER VARIETIES
Zantedeschia aethiopica 'Crowborough': A better variety, with more flowers. Other, more strongly-coloured flower species are not winter hardy, and are best overwintered in a glass house.

SUB-TROPICAL MARGINALS

Canna longwood
These come in a number of different varieties, including 'Endeavour', 'Ra', and 'Taney', which has canary-yellow

flowers, and 'Erebus', which has salmon-pink flowers. These can be chosen only if you have a greenhouse (glasshouse) for overwintering. Some of these varieties are difficult to obtain.

PLANTING MARGINAL PLANTS
When planting marginals, there are a few simple things to remember:

• What depth of water will the plant tolerate over the crown?
• What is the best soil for each plant?
• How large will the plant grow?

Not all plants are the same. Some need humus-rich soil and some will grow in plain gravel with no soil at all. If the plant grows very tall, it will need a larger basket to add weight, to stop it toppling over in windy weather.

> *Tip: Do not use sharp gravel. Any gravel that falls into the pond could damage the liner if trodden on.*

Fill the appropriately sized pond basket with 2 to 3 cm (about 1 inch) of gravel, then add aquatic soil to the halfway level. Place the plant into the basket with the crown 3 to 4 cm (1.5 to 2 inches) below the top and add soil (and fertilizer if required) up to this point. Pack down the soil to fill any voids, then top off with 10 to 20 mm (0.4 to 0.8 inches) of washed, rounded gravel.

Water the finished basket to wash away any surplus soil before you place it in the pond. If the water is deeper than the basket, young plants may drown. To avoid this, place the basket on bricks to raise the plants above the water until they are established. Then the bricks can be removed.

SUBMERGED AND OXYGENATING PLANTS
You need these to balance the oxygen/nitrogen within the pond, but just how many is a matter of contention. Two plants per square metre/yard is a rough guide. If you add fewer, it will take longer to reach the required balance, more will get you there quicker.

ROSEWARNE LEARNING CENTRE

When buying oxygenating plants, make sure they are a good, even colour, without dead tips or rotting stems. The plants should have new growth showing at the tips, and, in the case of bunched plants, look for small white roots – a sign that they are growing. All 'lead' weights should be removed, as they are not necessary when the oxygenators are planted.

Apart from *Myriophyllum spicatum*, all oxygenating plants will do better when planted in the correct baskets with soil and gravel. The old maxim 'throw them in tied to a stone' is a waste of time unless you have a natural pond, as the reason the plants have roots is to root into soil, not a pond liner. The other consideration is that fish will inevitably eat the young growth, and this will include the roots.

Aponogeton distachyos
Common name: Water Hawthorn.
Conditions: Deep water up to 1 metre (3 feet). Good, rich heavy soil.
Position: Full sun to get flowers.
Propagation: Seed or division of rhizome in summer.
Description: The water hawthorn sends up sweet-smelling flowers as early as late winter and will continue until late autumn (fall) with a small break in mid-summer. This makes it a good plant to mix with water lilies (see below). The large oval leaves offer cover for the fish and shade in the summer, helping to keep the pond cool. It is very easy to grow, and is one of the few strongly scented flowers in the pond.

OTHER VARIETIES
Aponogeton distachyos grandiflorum: As the normal plant, but with larger white flowers.

Callitriche stagnalis
Common name: Water Starwort.
Conditions: Pond soil with a water depth of up to 1 metre (40 ins).
Position: Sun to semi-shade.
Propagation: Division. Cut off young shoots and plant.
Description: The star-shaped rosettes of leaves float on the surface and thin roots descend to the bottom of the pond. A

very good oxygenator, but not suitable for natural ponds as it will take over. Best grown in a container of heavy clay soil. Prefers cold, deeper water. Bears very small, light green flowers in late summer.

Ceratophyllum demersum
Common name: Hornwort.
Conditions: Floating plant.
Position: Full sun to semi-shade.
Description: Although a native plant, it is quite difficult to grow as it likes still, nutrient-rich water. Once established, it will grow quickly and excess will need to be removed. This is easy, as it forms no roots and just floats around the pond. Many fish use it to spawn on, so it is useful if you intend to breed fish. Pinch out tips in winter, leave in pond, and new plants will grow in the spring. Remove excess plant material before the cold weather sets in.

Eleocharis acicularis
Common name: Hairgrass.
Conditions: Pond soil to a depth of 40 cm (15 inches).
Position: Sun to semi-shade.
Propagation: Division.
Description: Often sold as a tropical plant (the tropical variety is *Eleocharis acicularis*), it grows well in the margins of ponds. In its correct place, on the bottom of the pond, it is a reasonable oxygenator that produces an underwater lawn. It is very easy to propagate – just divide up the plants and pot up in spring. Fish love spawning on it, and, in the shallows, it also provides a great nursery for the fry.

Elodea canadensis
Common name: Canadian Pond Weed or Water Thyme.
Conditions: Pond soil with a water depth of up to 1 metre (40 ins).
Position: Sun to semi-shade.
Propagation: Division. Cut off young shoots and plant.
Description: Without doubt, one of the best oxygenators you can obtain. It can grow at an alarming rate in good conditions, so it is best contained in pots. Fish enjoy eating the younger

shoots, and it competes with algae for nutrients so it helps to keep water clear.

Hottonia palustris

Common name: Water Violet.

Conditions: Lime-free pond soil with a water depth of 60 cm (24 inches).

Position: Sun to semi-shade.

Description: The water violet is not a particularly good oxygenator, but it more than makes up for this with its bright green, feathery foliage and spike of violet-coloured flowers in early summer. Not an easy plant to establish as it can be fussy over conditions. Needs protecting from fish until it has grown to a reasonable size, as fish tend to dig it up.

Lagarosiphon major/Elodea crispa

Conditions: Pond soil with a water depth of up to 1 metre (40 inches).

Position: Sun to semi-shade.

Propagation: Division. Cut off young shoots and plant.

Description: Like *E. canadensis,* this is a very quick grower and should be contained in planting baskets. As the plant matures, it becomes untidy and does best if new plants are grown every two years. To grow new plants, pinch out the top 4 cm (1.5 inches) and pot up in shallow water in spring. As they root and start to grow, remove and replace older plants in the pond. Can be difficult to obtain.

Ludwigia palustris

Conditions: Rich, loamy soil.

Position: Sunny, shallow water.

Propagation: Tip cuttings in summer-growing period.

Description: A native of Britain, it has small red-brown leaves in pairs up the stem. It will grow only in warm, shallow water up to 40 cm (16 inches) deep, but it will adapt to surface growing and is excellent for covering the edge of the pond.

OTHER VARIETIES

Ludwigia grandiflora: A fast-growing species with bright yellow flowers in late summer. Can spread to 5 metres (15 feet) across, so cut back as necessary during the summer. Not fully hardy, so cut back in winter and grow cuttings in frost-free greenhouse.

Myriophyllum spicatum
Common name: Water Milfoil.
Conditions: Pond soil with a water depth of up to 1 metre (40 inches).
Position: Sun to semi-shade.
Propagation: Division. Cut off young shoots and plant.
Description: Needs lime-free water to flourish, but will tolerate low- to medium-hard water. The feathery bronze foliage spreads in loose mats beneath the surface, and, in summer, small green flowers are held above the water. *M. aquaticum* (parrot's feather) is the best-known variety and by far the quickest grower. It heads straight for the surface and grows across it – something of a pest! Nevertheless, it is good for new ponds as it provides instant cover while other plants catch up. Remove when more desirable plants have established themselves.

Nymphoides peltata
Common name: Fringed Water Lily.
Conditions: Pond soil with a water depth of up to 1 metre (40 inches).
Position: Sun to semi-shade.
Description: The fringed water lily is ideal for ponds where 'true' water lilies will not grow, such as those with moving water or fountains. Given the chance, it will quickly cover the surface and needs regular removal of excess foliage. Small yellow flowers appear in early summer. Remove the dead flowers to stop it setting seed and it will produce more flowers into autumn (fall). Not suitable for clay ponds as it can take over and is very difficult to clear.

Orontium aquaticum
Common name: Golden Club.
Conditions: Pond soil with a water depth of up to 40 cm (15 inches).

Position: Sun to semi-shade.
Propagation: Division. Cut off young shoots and plant.
Description: The golden club is often overlooked, as the long wait for maturity puts people off. However, it is very hardy and deserves a place in the water garden. The large spear-shaped leaves surround the long, white stems with golden spikes at the tip in early spring.

Potamogeton crispus
Common name: Pondweed.
Conditions: Pond soil with a water depth of up to 1 metre (40 inches).
Position: Sun to semi-shade.
Propagation: Division. Cut off young shoots and plant.
Description: Looking more like seaweed than a freshwater plant, *Potamogeton crispus* is an excellent oxygenator that needs to be in moving water to be at its best. It never threatens to take over the pond, so it is a good choice for those who want to keep maintenance to a minimum. In shaded ponds, the soft foliage is green, but in sunny areas it turns bronze.

Ranunculus aquatilis
Common name: Water Crow's Foot
Conditions: Pond soil with a water depth of up to 1 metre (40 inches).
Position: Sun to semi-shade.
Propagation: Division. Cut off young shoots and plant.
Description: Water Crow's Foot is an odd plant, as it has two types of leaves – a feathery submerged one and a clover-type leaf on the surface. In early summer, small white flowers with yellow centres are held just above the water's surface. The only drawback is that the plant dies back after flowering, but, all things considered, this is a small price to pay for a flowering oxygenator. Not invasive, and a good plant for shallower ponds.

Utricularia vulgaris
Common name: Bladderwort.
Conditions: Floating plant.

Description: One of the few insectivorous plants you can purchase for the pond, it is a good oxygenator but requires particular conditions to do well. It needs warm, acid water and a good supply of small invertebrates, which it captures in the submerged bladders. In late summer, small, golden-yellow flowers are held above water. Grow it if you can, as it is becoming more rare with every passing year.

WATER LILIES

More emphasis is placed on water lilies than any other pond plants, and yet most are purchased on price rather than suitability. In general, the cheaper the plant, the easier and quicker it will grow. A good example is Nymphaca alba, without doubt the best-selling water lily because it mutiplies so quickly and is cheaper than almost all others. However, it is totally unsuitable for anything but the largest pond or lake. It can, and does, take over ponds so completely that it displaces all the other plants and often the fish as well! In shallow water, it will grow up to 60 cm (2 feet) above the water level just to get more leaves to the light. Therefore, when purchasing your water lilies, be very careful and choose wisely.

TIPS FOR BUYING WATER LILIES

- *Always buy when in flower. If the plant is not in flower, it is very difficult to tell which species it is.*
- *Leaf size is not an indication of species. Small leaves may mean a young plant.*
- *There should be roots protruding from the basket. If there are no roots, it could have been potted up recently and it might not grow.*
- *Leaves should be an even green all over. Some have red or white variegated leaves, but the green should still be even.*
- *The rhizome should be clean, with no soft areas or black slime (which indicates fungus or crown rot). Remember, you cannot treat water plants in the pond as the treatment could kill the fish or other wildlife.*
- *The plant basket should be clean and free from blanket weed, duck weed and other pest plants.*
- *There should be no fish in with the plants or you could transfer disease to your own fish.*

- *Only buy plants in the correct baskets and displayed under water. Water lilies sold in plastic see-through packaging often have no leaves and a fungal infection. If you have other lilies this could spread.*
- *Check the leaves for any pests. They are normally on the underside.*

WHITE WATER LILIES

Nymphaea alba
Flower colour/period: Large white flowers with yellow stamens. Early summer to autumn (fall).
Size: Very large.
Maximum water depth: 2 metres (6 feet).
Comments: Best suited to deep, large ponds.

Nymphaea alba 'Plenissima'
Flower colour/period: Snow-white flowers with yellow centres. Early summer to autumn (fall).
Size: Large.
Maximum water depth: 1 metre (3 feet).
Comments: Very vigorous grower, best left for lakes.

Nymphaea candida
Flower colour/period: Small, compact snow-white flowers with rounded petals and yellow centres. Early summer to autumn.
Size: Medium.
Maximum water depth: 60 cm (2 feet)
Comments: Elegant plant for medium ponds.

Nymphaea 'Candidissima'
Flower colour/period: White with yellow centres. Early summer to autumn (fall).
Size: Medium.
Maximum water depth: 60 cm (2 feet).
Comments: Strong grower, but suitable for medium ponds. Very attractive apple-green foliage.

Nymphaea 'Caroliniana Nivea'
Flower colour/period: Very pretty stellate white. Early summer to autumn (fall).

Size: Small to medium.
Maximum water depth: 80 cm (5 feet, 6 inches).
Comments: Scented flowers held above the water surface.

Nymphaea 'Gladstoniana'

Flower colour/period: Large, paper-white flowers with yellow centres. Early summer to autumn (fall).
Size: Very large.
Maximum water depth: 1 metre (3 feet).
Comments: Similar to N. alba, but with better flowers. Should be left to larger ponds and lakes.

Nymphaea 'Gonnère'

Flower colour/period: Double-white, chrysanth-like flowers. Early summer to autumn (fall).
Size: Medium.
Maximum water depth: 1 metre (3 feet).
Comments: The best white water lily with the most beautiful flowers – a must!

Nymphaea 'Hermine'

Flower colour/period: White tulip-shaped flowers. Early summer to autumn (fall).
Size: Medium to large.
Maximum water depth: 60 cm (2 feet).
Comments: A very good white lily with slightly pointed, dark green leaves.

Nymphaea 'Lactea'

Flower colour/period: Fragrant white flowers with a pinkish blush. Early summer to autumn (fall).
Size: Small to medium.
Maximum water depth: 40 cm (16 inches).
Comments: A truly graceful flower that does best in warm, shallow water. In colder climates, you may need to lower it to deeper water in winter.

Nymphaea 'Marliacea Alba'

Flower colour/period: Scented white flowers. Early summer to

autumn (fall).
Size: Medium.
Maximum water depth: 60 cm (2 feet).
Comments: A well-known group of liles, prized for their scented flowers and trouble-free growing. Not available everywhere.

Nymphaea 'Marliacea Albida'
Flower colour/period: Scented white flowers. Early summer to autumn (fall).
Size: Medium to large.
Maximum water depth: 80 cm (32 inches).
Comments: A prolific plant that is also very free-flowering. Best for larger ponds.

Nymphaea 'Maxima'
Flower colour/period: Pure-white, peony-shaped flowers. Early summer to autumn (fall).
Size: Large.
Maximum water depth: 50 to 60 cm (20 to 24 inches).
Comments: Beautiful, apple-green foliage. Flowers well early in the season, followed by masses of foliage. Good for surface cover but is not free-flowering.

Nymphaea odorata minor alba
Flower colour/period: Tiny white flowers with yellow centres. Early summer to autumn (fall).
Size: Small.
Maximum water depth: 30 cm (12 inches).
Comments: Ideal for the patio pond, as it not only stays small but is also prolific. Best in a shallow, sunny position.

Nymphaea odorata 'Walter Pagels'
Flower colour/period: Blush-white flowers. Early summer to autumn (fall).
Size: Small.
Maximum water depth: 30 cm (12 inches).
Comments: Pretty white flowers and a carpet of small, mid-green leaves make this a prized plant for the smaller wildlife or patio pond. It can be difficult to obtain.

Nymphaea tetragona 'Georgi'
Flower colour/period: Small, white flowers. Early summer to autumn (fall).
Size: Miniature to small.
Maximum water depth: 30 cm (12 inches).
Comments: Another patio lily, prolific and relatively free-flowering in a sunny position.

YELLOW WATER LILIES

Nymphaea 'Colonel A.J. Welch'
Flower colour/period: Bright yellow held above the water's surface. Early summer to autumn (fall).
Size: Medium.
Maximum water depth: 80 cm (32 inches).
Comments: Not as popular as it deserves to be. It is more reliable than *Nymphaea marliacea chromatella* and has smaller leaves with red variegation.

Nymphaea 'Joey Tomocik'
Flower colour/period: Stunning, deep-yellow glossy petals. Early summer to autumn (fall).
Size: Large.
Maximum water depth: 75 cm (30 inches).
Comments: Flowers best when planted in a large pond or lake without a container.

Nyphaea 'Lemon Chiffon'
Flower colour/period: Deep, semi-double. Early summer to autumn.
Size: Small to medium.
Maximum water depth: 50 cm (20 inches).
Comments: The leaves are mid-green with darker-green flecks. It is ideal for the smaller water garden, but often difficult to find.

Nymphaea 'Marliacea Chromatella'
Flower colour/period: Canary-yellow with the outer petals blushed pink at the base. Early summer to autumn (fall).
Size: Large and vigorous.
Maximum water depth: 2 metres (6 feet).

Comments: The most popular yellow lily, but for the wrong reasons. It grows very quickly and can be as much of a problem as *Nymphaea alba*. With leaves measuring up to 45 cm (18 inches) across, *Nymphaea 'Marliacea Chromatella'* is too large for all but the biggest and deepest ponds. It is also susceptible to crown rot.

Nymphaea 'Moorei'
Flower colour/period: Straw-coloured and free-flowering. Early summer to autumn (fall).
Size: Medium to large.
Maximum water depth: 60 cm (2 feet).
Comments: Often sold as *Nymphaea marliacea chromatella* but the flowers are not as yellow and it is not as vigorous.

Nymphaea 'Odorata Sulphurea'
Flower colour/period: Large, sulphur-yellow flowers held above the water's surface. Early summer to autumn (fall).
Size: Small to medium.
Maximum water depth: 40 cm (16 inches).
Comments: A very good lily, free-flowering and not too vigorous. Well suited to medium-sized ponds.

Nymphaea 'Odorata Sulphurea Grandiflora'
Flower colour/period: Very large, sulphur-yellow flowers held above the water. Early summer to autumn (fall).
Size: Medium.
Maximum water depth: 50 cm (20 inches).
Comments: As its name suggests, it has larger flowers than *Nymphaea odorata sulphurea* (see above) and grows slightly larger.

Nymphaea 'Pygmaea Helvola'
Flower colour/period: Very small, canary-yellow flowers. Early summer to autumn (fall).
Size: Pygmy to small.
Maximum water depth: 20 cm (8 inches).
Comments: The perfect lily for the water feature with no fish, but needs protecting from very cold weather.

Nymphaea 'Sunrise'
Flower colour/period: Immense flowers of lemon-yellow (inspiring its name). Each flower has a crimped edge to it, which can measure up to 30 cm (1 foot) across. Early summer to autumn (fall).
Size: Medium to large.
Maximum water depth: 80 cm (32 inches).
Comments: If you have the space, 'Sunrise' is a must. With its fantastic flowers held over red, variegated leaves, it makes a striking addition to any pond.

Nymphaea 'Texas Dawn'
Flower colour/period: The flowers are a glorious mid-yellow colour with a blush peach around the base. Early summer to autumn (fall).
Size: Medium to large.
Maximum water depth: 1 metre (3 feet).
Comments: One of my favourite lilies, it has a tropical look and is very hardy. *Nymphaea 'Texas Dawn'* has one of the longest flowering periods of any lily I have grown, and is a must if you have the space.

Nymphaea 'Yellow Princess'
Flower colour/period: Pale yellow. Early summer to autumn (fall).
Size: Medium.
Maximum water depth: 60 cm (2 feet).
Comments: Another more unusual variety, not often seen for sale but worthwhile if you come across it. Glossy green leaves with a light specking.

PINK WATER LILIES

Nymphaea 'Amabilis'
Flower colour/period: Large, salmon-pink flowers with flesh-coloured sepals. Early summer to autumn (fall).
Size: Medium to large.
Maximum water depth: 1 metre (3 feet).
Comments: Nymphaea 'Amabilis' is a good free-flowering lily for the large pond.

Nymphaea 'American Star'
Flower colour/period: Blush-pink petals, deeper at base and fading to almost white at the tips. Early summer to autumn (fall).
Size: Medium.
Maximum water depth: Up to 50 cm (18 inches).
Comments: Beautiful star-shaped flowers. Profuse blooms with a pleasant fragrance.

Nymphaea 'Darwin'
Flower colour/period: Deep pink. Early summer to autumn (fall).
Size: Large.
Maximum water depth: 1 metre (3 feet).
Comments: Beautifully shaped flowers, quite rare.

Nymphaea 'Fabiola Mrs Richmond'
Flower colour/period: Large rosy flowers. Early summer to autumn (fall).
Size: Large.
Maximum water depth: 1 metre (3 feet).
Comments: For larger ponds only. Good for small lakes as it does not spread as fast as *Nymphaea carnea*.

Nymphaea 'Helen Fowler'
Flower colour/period: A stunning coral-pink flower with a sweet scent. Early summer to autumn (fall).
Size: Medium.
Maximum water depth: 50 cm (20 inches).
Comments: A wonderful flower set off by deep-green/purple leaves. Another favourite of mine. Quite slow to grow, but worth the wait. Free-flowering once settled.

Nymphaea 'Laydekeri Lilacea'
Flower colour/period: Small, lilac to pink flowers held above the water. Early summer to autumn (fall).
Size: Small.
Maximum water depth: 50 cm (18 inches).
Comments: Another plant suited to smaller patio ponds and features. Protect from frost in winter.

Nymphaea 'Livingstone'
Flower colour/period: Pink to light red, candy striped. Early summer to autumn (fall).
Size: Medium.
Maximum water depth: 40 cm (16 inches).
Comments: Needs a warm, sunny position to do well. Has an extraordinary serrated edge to its glossy green leaves.

Nymphaea 'Madame Wilfron Gonnère'
Flower colour/period: Soft pink, semi-double. Early summer to autumn (fall).
Size: Medium to large.
Maximum water depth: 1 metre (3 feet).
Comments: A wonderful lily, slow to mature, but worth the wait. Large round leaves add to the attraction of the double flower.

Nymphaea 'Marliacea Carnea'
Flower colour/period: Large and very pale. Almost white, flushed with pink. Early summer to autumn (fall).
Size: Very large.
Maximum water depth: 2 metres (6 feet).
Comments: Need plenty of space. Ideal for lakes.

Nymphaea 'Masaniello'
Flower colour/period: Very large, pink flowers. Early summer to autumn (fall).
Size: Large and vigorous.
Maximum water depth: 1 metre (3 feet).
Comments: Best suited to large ponds. It is very tough and will tolerate flowing water.

Nymphaea 'Neptune'
Flower colour/period: Large, with long petals that are pale pink on the outside and slightly deeper on the inside, with crimson stripes. Early summer to autumn (fall).
Size: Medium.
Maximum water depth: 60 cm (2 feet).
Comments: An unusual lily, rare but interesting.

Nymphaea odorata 'Caroliniana'
Flower colour/period: Flesh pink to salmon. Prolific bloomer. Early summer to autumn (fall).
Size: Medium.
Maximum water depth: 60 cm (2 feet).
Comments: Very pretty flower and a good, strong grower.

Nymphaea odorata 'Firecrest'
Flower colour/period: Very bright pink. Early summer to autumn (fall).
Size: Medium.
Maximum water depth: 60 cm (2 feet).
Comments: If you only buy one pink-flowered lily, this is should be it. Be careful, however, as several other varieties are sometimes sold as 'Firecrest', so only buy this lily when it is in flower. 'Firecrest' can be difficult to obtain.

Nymphaea odorata 'Rose Arey'
Flower colour/period: Stunning coral pink. Early summer to autumn (fall).
Size: Small to medium.
Maximum water depth: 60 cm (2 feet).
Comments: An old favourite, very easy to find in shops and superb for small ponds.

Nymphaea odorata 'William B. Shaw'
Flower colour/period: Pastel pink and fragrant. Early summer to autumn (fall).
Size: Medium.
Maximum water depth: 60 cm (2 feet).
Comments: Free-flowering variety that is hard to find, but worth the trouble.

Nymphaea 'Perry's Fire Opal'
Flower colour/period: Deep pink and double, standing above the water. Early summer to autumn (fall).
Size: Large.
Maximum water depth: 80 cm (32 inches).
Comments: Another quite rare variety, but the double flowers make it a worthy contender for pond space.

Nymphaea 'Pink Sensation'
Flower colour/period: Salmon pink flowers. Early summer to autumn (fall).
Size: Medium to large.
Maximum water depth: 60 cm (2 feet).
Comments: Strong growing and free-flowering.

Nymphaea 'Rose Magnolia'
Flower colour/period: Light pink fading to cream, with a wide span once open fully. Early summer to autumn (fall).
Size: Medium to large.
Maximum water depth: 60 cm (2 feet).
Comments: Very pretty and free-flowering.

Nymphaea 'Rossennymphe'
Flower colour/period: Star-shaped flowers fading from rose-pink to cream as they age. Early summer to autumn (fall).
Size: Medium to large.
Maximum water depth: 50 to 60 cm (20 to 24 inches).
Comments: 'Rossennymphe' flowers early in the season, flowering successively throughout. It has attractive foliage, with reddish leaves.

Nymphaea 'William Doogue'
Flower colour/period: Flesh pink. Early summer to autumn (fall).
Size: Medium.
Maximum water depth: 60 cm (2 feet).
Comments: A less-well-known variety, but worth the space in a larger pond.

RED WATER LILIES

Nymphaea 'Atropurpurea'
Flower colour/period: The beautiful red flowers are tinged on the edges with a deeper red, and set off with yellow anthers. Early summer to autumn (fall).
Size: Small to medium.
Maximum water depth: 60 cm (2 feet).
Comments: Beautiful maroon-and-green leaves.

Nymphaea 'Attraction'
Flower colour/period: Large, burgundy red with dark-red/brown stamens. Early summer to autumn (fall).
Size: Large.
Maximum water depth: 1 metre (3 feet).
Comments: A vigorous, attractive plant for larger ponds. Free-flowering.

Nymphaea 'Charles de Meurville'
Flower colour/period: This plant has very impressive, large vermilion-red flowers with orange stamens. Early summer to autumn (fall).
Size: Large.
Maximum water depth: 1 metre (3 feet).
Comments: Ideal in larger ponds as it has many flowers early in the season, so spreading the flowering period of the pond's lilies.

Nymphaea 'Conqueror'
Flower colour/period: Bright red flowers with dark red veins. Early summer to autumn (fall).
Size: Large.
Maximum water depth: 80 cm (32 inches).
Comments: For the larger pond only.

Nymphaea 'Ellisiana'
Flower colour/period: Medium, vermilion-red flowers with orange stamens. Early summer to autumn (fall).
Size: Small to medium,
Maximum water depth: 80 cm (32 inches).
Comments: A very beautiful lily for smaller ponds. When buying, see it in flower, as *Nymphaea laydekeri fulgens* is often sold in its place.

Nymphaea 'Escarboucle'
Flower colour/period: Carmine-red blooms, with yellow stamens. Early summer to autumn (fall).
Size: Medium to large.
Maximum water depth: 1 metre (3 feet).

Comments: Probably the best-known red water lily and rightly so. A must if you have the space.

Nymphaea 'Froebelii'
Flower colour/period: Prolific bloomer with clear, cherry-red flowers. Early summer to autumn (fall).
Size: Small to medium.
Maximum water depth: 45 cm (18 inches).
Comments: Very attractive red lily for smaller ponds. Does best in shallow, warm water.

Nymphaea 'James Brydon'
Flower colour/period: Double peony-shaped. Crimson with a tinge of pink. Early summer to autumn (fall).
Size: Medium to large.
Maximum water depth: 60 cm (2 feet).
Comments: The second-best, red water lily. An old favourite, and one of the few double lilies.

Nymphaea 'Laydekeri Fulgens'
Flower colour/period: Deep red, but can be pinkish in the early part of the season. Early summer to autumn (fall).
Size: Small to medium.
Maximum water depth: 60 cm (2 feet).
Comments: Free-flowering. Does best in shallow water.

Nymphaea 'Laydekeri Purpurata'
Flower colour/period: Dusky rose pink, although classified as red. Early summer to autumn (fall).
Size: Small to medium.
Maximum water depth: 40 cm (16 inches).
Comments: Very attractive foliage with dark purple markings. Very shallow water for the best results, but needs to be put in deeper water in winter.

Nymphaea 'Lucida'
Flower colour/period: Cardinal red. Early summer to autumn (fall).
Size: Medium.

Maximum water depth: 60 cm (2 feet).
Comments: A worthy lily, not often seen for sale, but a very reliable bloomer.

Nymphaea 'Newton'
Flower colour/period: Has brilliant-scarlet, star-shaped flowers. Free flowering. Early summer to autumn (fall).
Size: Medium to large.
Maximum water depth: 40 to 50 cm (15 to 20 inches).
Comments: Free-flowering. Flowers well throughout the season.

Nymphaea 'René Gérard'
Flower colour/period: Rose-pink bloom, splashed with crimson. Early summer to autumn (fall).
Size: Medium.
Maximum water depth: 40 to 50 cm (15 to 20 inches).
Comments: An attractive, colourful, free-flowering, traditional water lily.

Nymphaea 'Splendida'
Flower colour/period: Ruby-red flowers with orange stamens. Early summer to autumn (fall).
Size: Large.
Maximum water depth: 60 cm (24 inches).
Comments: The blooms deepen as the plant matures.

Nymphaea 'William Falconer'
Flower colour/period: Deep blood-red flowers. Early summer to autumn (fall).
Size: Small to medium.
Maximum water depth: 45 cm (18 inches).
Comments: Ideal for smaller ponds where there is only room for one lily, as *Nymphaea 'William Falconer'* has a long flowering season.

Nymphaea 'Wow'
Flower colour/period: Day-glo pink flowers stand above the water. Early summer to autumn (fall).

Size: Medium to large.
Maximum water depth: 1 metre (3 feet).
Comments: The name says it all – a marvellous plant, ideal for brightening up any water garden.

UNUSUAL LILY VARIETIES

Nymphaea 'Arc-en-Ciel'
Flower colour/period: White with a pale-pink blush. Early summer to autumn (fall).
Size: Medium to large.
Maximum water depth: 80 cm (32 inches).
Comments: Kept mainly for its leaves, which are purple-red when young, fading to green and white variegation. If you see it and have room in the pond, buy it.

Nymphaea 'Aurora'
Flower colour/period: Open orange but change to red within a few days. Early summer to autumn (fall).
Size: Small to medium.
Maximum water depth: 40 cm (16 inches).
Comments: Needs shallow, warm water to be at its best.

Nymphaea 'Comanche'
Flower colour/period: The inner petals change from apricot-yellow to copper-red, while the outer petals remain yellow. Early summer to autumn (fall).
Size: Medium.
Maximum water depth: 40 to 50 cm (16 to 20 inches).
Comments: Flowers better later in the season. The leaves are flecked with purple.

Nymphaea 'Odalisque'
Flower colour/period: Pink turning to white. Early summer to autumn (fall).
Size: Medium to large.
Maximum water depth: 1 metre (3 feet).
Comments: Good flowers held above the water's surface. Two lilies for the price of one.

Nymphaea 'Sioux'
Flower colour/period: Large, copper-coloured flowers, deepening with age. Early summer to autumn (fall).
Size: Medium.
Maximum water depth: 60 cm (2 feet).
Comments: Prolific bloomer. One of the best 'variable' lilies.

PLANTING WATER LILIES

When you get your water lily home, it should be already potted in the correct pond basket. However, if it needs repotting, follow the following steps.

You will need:
- Pond plant baskets (various sizes)
- Hessian or foam basket liners (optional)
- Aquatic soil
- 10- to 20-mm (0.4- to 0.8-inch) gravel
- A sharp knife
- Slow-release fertilizer tablets. You can buy these specifically for water plants. They should be low in nitrogen, which stimulates leaf growth rather than flowers.

STEP-BY-STEP INSTRUCTIONS

- Take the lily from its container and remove all the soil from the roots. Trim to remove the dead or damaged roots and any old leaves. Check the rhizome for any soft areas and remove them. If the plant has more than one crown, you can split the lily into two plants. Ideally, each rhizome should be 10 to 15 cm (4 to 6 inches) long with roots along it.
- Select a basket to go with the lily you have chosen. A small lily will require a basket of 3 to 5 litres (0.5 to 1 UK gallons or 0.8 to 1.3 US fluid gallons), a medium lily 10 to 15 litres (2.25 to 3.25 UK gallons or 2.5 to 4 US fluid gallons), and a large lily 15 litres (3.25 UK gallons or 4 US fluid gallons) or larger. If you are unable to find a basket large enough, you can use a washing basket lined with glass house shading to prevent the soil from falling. If the basket has large holes, you will need a liner.
- Fill half the basket with soil and spread the roots across it. Holding the rhizome, fill the basket to within 3 to 5 cm (1.5 to 2 inches) of the top. The rhizome should now be sitting on the

surface of the soil. Insert a slow-release fertilizer tablet.
- Fill the rest of the basket with washed gravel. If you keep koi or other large fish, you may need to use larger pebbles to stop them digging up the plants.
- Before you place the lily in the pond, water it well. This will wash away any excess soil and stop it clouding the pond.
- The lily should be placed with the leaves around 5 cm (2 inches) below the surface, and lowered slowly as the plant grows until the required depth is reached.

> *Tip: If the pond is too deep to begin with, stand the plant on an upturned pond basket or plastic plant pot. Avoid using bricks or concrete blocks as they can damage the pond liner and pollute the water with lime. Fish can, and will, scratch themselves on them.*

FLOATING PLANTS

Floating plants are often overlooked, but they do have a place in the pond, although some are a pest and may take over to the point of killing off submerged plants. Most of them can be controlled by simply removing excess plant material as and when necessary.

Many of the more decorative plants are not hardy below 10 degrees Celsius (50 degrees Fahrenheit), and should be removed before the first cold weather fronts set in, to ensure they survive for the following season. Usually, floating plants are treated as aquatic bedding plants and are replaced every year in spring after the last frost.

Some floating plants are classed as pests and should not be grown. The water hyacinth *(Eichhornia crassipes),* for example, is a prohibited plant in most water climate zones as it multiplies so fast it can clog rivers and lakes. Check with your local authority if you are uncertain about a plant.

Eichhornia crassipes
Common name: Water Hyacinth.
Conditions: Floating plant.
Position: Full sun to semi-shade.
Description: A very-fast-growing plant in the correct conditions

(i.e. warm, nutrient-rich water). The plant is made up from leaves with a large, air-filled base that in turn leads up a thin stalk to a rounded, glossy green leaf. In warm climates, the plant will also send up a flower spike of pale lavender flowers with a darker centre. The topmost petal is also marked with a yellow spot, with a dark blue surround. They are ideal for growing in cool climates in which they are killed off in winter. They work very well as vegetable filters, absorbing vast amounts of nitrogen (in the form of nitrate) from the water, which in turn reduces algae growth. They are also good for removing heavy metals (e.g. copper) from the water, so they are a useful filter for heavily stocked garden ponds and koi ponds. They are also useful as a food for koi and are often used as a spawning medium.

Hydrocharis morsus-ranae
Common name: Frog Bit.
Conditions: Floating plant.
Position: Full sun to semi-shade.
Description: Frog bit is ideal for the half-barrel water feature or for the small wildlife pond. Slow to appear in early summer, the small, round fleshy leaves start to spread out, later to be followed by white flowers. In early autumn (fall), the frog bit drops resting buds to the bottom ready for next year. Its season is short, but the small, lily-like foliage and flowers are a welcome addition.

Lemna species
Common name: Duck Weed.
Conditions: Floating plant.
Position: Full sun to semi-shade.
Description: Duck weed is probably the second biggest pest, after blanket weed, in garden ponds. It grows at an incredible rate and seems unstoppable. Nevertheless, it is quite useful in providing cover. There are four main species of duck weed:

- **Lemna gibba:** Gibberous duck weed is similar to *L. minor*, with small, oval leaves measuring 3 to 7 mm (0.1 to 0.3 inches) across and a single root. The underside of the leaf is very convex.
- **Lemna minor:** Lesser duck weed is identified by small, glossy

round or oval leaves measuring 4 to 8 mm (0.2 to 0.3 inches) across, with a single root hanging underneath.

- **Lemna polyrhiza:** Greater duck weed is the largest of the species and grows leaves measuring 10 to 20 mm (0.4 to 0.8 inches) across, with up to 16 roots hanging down. The underside of the leaves are sometimes reddish in colour.
- **Lemna trisulca:** Ivy-leafed duck weed has pointed leaves measuring 6 to 12 mm (0.25 to 0.4 inches) long, which are a pale green. They are usually submerged for most of the season, floating during the flowering period only. The younger plants bud from the parent leaf and stay attached until disturbed. It prefers clear, alkaline water.

Pistia stratiotes
Common name: Water Lettuce.
Conditions: Floating plant.
Position: Full sun to semi-shade.
Description: The water lettuce is really a tropical plant that is sold as an aquatic bedding plant. It cannot survive cold winters. It looks like a lettuce, with thick, pale-green corrugated leaves. It likes warm, shallow water with little or no movement. A mass of fine roots hang under the plant and are ideal as a floating hide for rearing young fish. It reproduces by budding off new plants from runners that appear from under the plant. As it grows, remove excess plants.

Rorippa nasturtium aquaticum
Common Name: 'True' Water Cress.
Conditions: Floating plant.
Position: Full sun to semi-shade.
Description: This plant has stems that float in the water and creep over the surrounding ground. It grows tiny (4 mm or less than a quarter of an inch), pretty white flowers, each of which has four petals. It is often cultivated for its pepper-flavoured leaves, which are high in vitamins A and C.

Stratiotes aloides
Common name: Water Soldier.
Conditions: Floating plant.

Position: Full sun to semi-shade.
Description: The water soldier looks like a pineapple top and has similar serrated edges. It does best in cold water. In summer, it floats to the surface and occasionally sends up white flowers by mid-summer. Later, it sinks to the bottom and roots for the winter, during which it acts as an oxygenator. It reproduces by sending out runners that break away when mature.

Trapa natans
Common name: Water Chestnut.
Conditions: Floating plant.
Position: Full sun to semi-shade.
Description: The water chestnut is an annual floating plant found in temperate climates.

BOG PLANTS
These are not pond plants in the true sense, but planting them around the pond gives you the chance to spread the water garden over a greater area. This provides useful extra colour if you are limited in your choice of pond plants by the fish you keep.

A simple bog garden can be set up by using the offcuts from the pond liner to line a shallow excavation, which can then be perforated to allow excess water to drain out of the bog garden area. The liner can be filled with a rich humus-and-soil mix. Do not use plain peat, as the plants will not grow, and any runoff into the pond will affect the water chemistry. The best mix is sterilised topsoil, well-rotted leaf mould, and a little charcoal. Try not to use potting composts or soil which has fertilizers added. The fertilizer will run into the pond creating green water and algae growth.

Most bog plants are normal garden plants that prefer wet or very moist soil, so, if you have these conditions, it may not be necessary to use a liner under the bog area.

Cardamine pratensis
Common name: Bitter Cress, Lady's Mantle, and Milk Maid.
Conditions: Damp to bog, up to 5 cm (2 inches) water depth.
Position: Full sun to semi-shade.

Propagation: Seed or leaf-tip cuttings.
Description: A hardy perennial, which spreads with a creeping rhizome. Long stems of pale pink flower-sprays in late spring or early summer, held above long-stemmed leaves. It grows up to a height of 40 cm (16 inches).

OTHER VARIETIES
Cardamine p. 'Flore Pleno': Double form with pale mauve flowers, more compact than the single version.
Cardamine trifolia: Pinky mauve flowers held well above the foliage. Ideal for edging the pond.

Filipendula ulmaria
Common name: Meadowsweet.
Conditions: Damp to bog, up to 5 cm (2 inches) water depth.
Position: Full sun to semi-shade.
Propagation: Rhizome division or cuttings.
Description: A very hardy perennial that grows up to 2 metres (6 feet) tall in sheltered areas. In late summer, clusters of cream-to-white scented flowers are held above the green leaves. It grows from a creeping rhizome and spreads slowly along the edge of the water.

OTHER VARIETIES
Filipendula ulmaria 'Aurea': The seldom-seen golden form that does best in shade. It grows to a height of 1 metre (3 feet).

Gunnera manicata
Common name: Giant Rhubarb.
Conditions: Wet to sodden in deep, rich soil.
Position: Full sun to semi-shade, but must be sheltered from strong winds.
Propagation: Crown division or propagation of suckers.
Description: Although one of the most sought-after plants, it rarely does well in gardens as it requires a large area to be at its best and it is not particularly hardy. Unless well protected in winter, it will die back, and this stops it reaching its optimum size. In the right position, it can grow leaves measuring up to 2 metres (6 feet) across. It needs a mulch of well-rotted manure

every year to promote growth over winter, when it should be covered with at least 30 cm (12 inches) of straw to protect it from the cold.

OTHER VARIETIES
Gunnera tinctoria syn. chilensis: The giant Chilean rhubarb is not as large – the leaves measure only 1 metre (3 feet) across – yet the plant can grow up to 2 metres (6 feet) tall. It is hardier and better suited to the garden.

Impatiens glandulifera
Common name: Indian Balsam.
Conditions: Damp to 5 cm (2 inches) water depth.
Position: Full sun to shade.
Propagation: Needs no help. Self-seeds anywhere.
Description: This plant will be a pest in most gardens if left unchecked, as it spreads quickly in any damp soil. It grows up to 2 metres (6 feet) tall and is covered with rose pink or purple helmet-shaped flowers in mid to late summer. Dead-head it as it flowers to prevent it setting seed and spreading.

Iris ensata kaempferi 'Rose Queen'
Common name: Japanese Flag.
Conditions: Does best in any moist, peat-rich soil.
Position: Sun or semi-shade.
Propagation: Seed not true to form. Division in summer.
Description: Beautiful, large rose-pink flowers appear late in the season on a tall stem above lush green foliage. It is really a bog plant, but it can tolerate 4 cm (1.75 inches) of water when mature. An essential addition for the keen water gardener.

OTHER VARIETIES
Iris k. 'Lady In Waiting': A rare form with white flowers blushed purple, with a purple edge and a golden-yellow-tinged green throat.

Lysimachia clethroides
Common name: Loosestrife.
Conditions: Any damp soil except alkaline.

Position: Any.
Propagation: Rhizome division or seed.
Description: An excellent plant to grow, as it attracts butterflies to the pond. It spreads by creeping rhizome and grows up to 80 cm (32 inches). Spear-shaped bunches of white flowers are held on long stems in late summer and early autumn (fall).

Petasites officinalis
Common name: Petasites.
Conditions: Moist soil.
Position: Shady and protected, as the wind tears the leaves.
Propagation: Seed and root division.
Description: A hardy perennial from Europe and Japan, it has scented, pink-to-violet flowers in late winter, with leaves produced later. The leaves are the shape of elephant ears and measure up to 60 cm (2 feet) across. Mainly grown for its decorative leaves, it is an excellent alternative to *Gunnera manicata,* as it requires little maintenance and is winter-hardy. It grows to a height of 1.2 metres (3 feet, 8 inches). It may be difficult to obtain.

OTHER VARIETIES
Petasites fragrans: A dwarf species with fragrant pink flowers, which grows to a height of 30 cm (12 inches).
Petasites japonicus: This variety is shorter again – up to 25 cm (10 inches), with large, round leaves below yellow flowers.

Potentilla palustris
Common name: Marsh Potentilla.
Conditions: Damp to 15 cm (6 inches) of water.
Position: Sunny, to get the best from the autumn (fall) colour.
Propagation: Divison of crown, or stem cuttings.
Description: An attractive plant, once very common but now quite rare. The leaves are pale green and arranged in the shape of a hand. They turn bright crimson in the autumn. The flowers are reddish-brown and appear in mid-summer.

OTHER VARIETIES
Potentilla anserina: Silver weed is a ground-covering species.

The leaves are a blue-green colour ranging to silver, and have up to 25 leaflets. Large yellow flowers, measuring 2 to 3 cm (1 to 1.5 inches) across, appear throughout the season. It grows to a height of 15 to 50 cm (6 to 20 inches).

Primula

Conditions: Damp to wet, good rich soil. Mulch every two years and feed plants annually.
Position: Sun or semi shade.
Propagation: Clump division after flowering.
Description: One of the most popular plants for the bog garden, offering colour from late winter to mid-summer. The colours are always strong, and, as new hybrids appear, the variety increases every year. The current popular species include:

- **Primula beesiana:** A mauve-flowered species that grows up to 70 cm (28 inches) tall and self-seeds.
- **Primula bulleyana:** With orange flowers.
- **Primula denticulata:** Large balls of flowers held on a long stem in red, white, purple and mauve colours.
- **Primula florindae:** The giant cowslip measuring up to 90 cm (34 inches) tall, with bright yellow flowers in early summer. Does best in semi shade with moist, acidic conditions.
- **Primula prolifera:** A tall species that reaches a height of 1 metre (3 feet) with deep yellow flowers.
- **Primula japonica:** The Japanese primula has a large variety of flower colours, ranging from pink to blue. It looks best in large plantings.
- **Primula rosea 'Royle'/splendeus:** This variety comes from Tibet. It has reddish-pink flowers with yellow centres.
- **Primula vialii:** A red, conical-shaped flower spike that opens up with purple/violet-coloured flowers.

Rheum palmatum

Common name: Ornamental Rhubarb.
Conditions: Needs rich, moist soil. Mulch every year with well-rotted manure.
Position: Sun or semi-shade out of the wind, to avoid damage to the leaves.

Propagation: Crown division in spring.
Description: Another gunnera substitute, this is much smaller and probably better, as it is hardy and needs no winter protection. It is also quick-growing, with leaves measuring up to 90 cm (32 inches) across. In the summer, it produces a flower spike up to 3 metres (9 feet) tall, with pink to purple flowers.

CULTIVARS
Rheum palmatum 'Atrosanguineum': An attractive cultivar with foliage that is finely cut and very red in early spring. The flowers are violet to red in colour.
Rheum palmatum 'Bowles Crimson': As above, but with a white flower.
Rheum palmatum tanguticum: A larger-growing species measuring up to 2.4 metres (7 feet) tall with a red flower.

Rodgersia aesculifolia 'Batalin'
Common name: Rodgersia.
Conditions: Rich moist soil and regular feeds.
Position: Can be grown in shade or semi-shade only, as the sun burns the leaves very quickly.
Propagation: Seed or crown division.
Description: A wonderful plant from the Far East. It has large panicles of white held above leaves similar to those of a horse chestnut, which are a rich, dark green. It can grow to 1.5 metres (5 feet) tall, so it needs space to achieve its full potential.

OTHER VARIETIES
Rodgersia pinnata: Similar to *R. aesculifolia*, but smaller – measuring up to 1 metre (3 feet) tall.
Rodgersia podophylla: Large leaves with a satin-bronze finish, which fade to green as the season progresses. Large pyramids of white flowers in mid-summer.
Rodgersia sambucifolia: With large, beautiful, deeply cut leaves, this makes a statement in the bog garden. It is followed by white flowers in summer.
Rodgersia pinnata 'Superba': A cultivar with bronze foliage and purple flowers.

Schizostylis coccinea
Common name: Kaffir Lily.
Conditions: Damp, rich soil.
Position: Full sun.
Propagation: From offshoots of main clump.
Description: One of the few bog plants to flower late in the season, it brings a welcome splash of colour to the pond surround. Beautiful, bright pink flowers are held above long, narrow, mid-green leaves. May be difficult to obtain.

CULTIVARS
Schizostylis coccinea alba: A very fine, white-flowered cultivar.
Schizostylis coccinea 'Major': Larger pink flowers than *Schizostylis coccinea*.
Schizostylis coccinea 'Sunset': Salmon-pink flowers.
Schizostylis coccinea var: A cultivar seen for sale under various names, which can make it difficult to obtain. It has bright red flowers.

Sisyrinchium species
Conditions: Damp soil to 5 cm (2 inches) water depth.
Position: Full sun.
Propagation: Seed or clump division.
Description: Almost a miniature iris. It has short, narrow, mid-green leaves that measure up to 30 cm (12 inches) long. In late summer, it has small flowers held above the leaves. It forms small clumps and spreads by self-seeding.

OTHER VARIETIES
Sisyrinchium bellum: Pale mauve flowers held up on a thin, wiry stem.
Sisyrinchium 'Biscutella': Buff-coloured flowers on wiry stems.
Sisyrinchium boreale: Yellow flowers.
Sisyrinchium 'E.K. Balls': Small mauve flowers similar to an iris.

CHAPTER 5

PUMPS

1. Submersible pumps
2. External pumps
3. Calculating flow rate
4. Choosing your pump
5. Pump maintenance

Unless you are very lucky and you have a spring in your garden to provide water movement, you will need a pump. This area of pondkeeping is the most difficult to negotiate for the new water gardener, as there is such a bewildering number of filters and pumps available. You can buy pumps for filters only, fountains only, filters and fountains combined, and pumps that can be in or out of the water.

In order to choose the right pump, you need to decide what you want to do with it. Prices vary from a few pounds or dollars to many hundreds, but the cheapest are generally not worth considering except as a spare or a back-up.

Whichever pump you decide on, it will fail one day, so you will need to have a spare. A cheap one will do until you can replace the original, but, whatever it costs, it will still be cheaper than buying a new collection of fish!

There are two basic types of pump – the submersible, which is installed underwater, and the external, which is mounted outside the pond in a dry location.

SUBMERSIBLE PUMPS

The most common type of submersible pump is the upright or sump pump. It is much cheaper to buy than other pumps, but expensive to run, as it consumes a lot of electricity. This pump may use as much as five times more energy than the most economical type.

The second type of submersible is often referred to as a filter pump. It has a larger filter area and much lower running costs. Some are designed for filtration only and are capable of pumping large solids without breaking or clogging. They require less maintenance because of this.

Fountain pumps are another submersible. They are capable of higher pressure and are, therefore, more suitable for fountains and ornaments, although they generally have a pre-filter foam that will clog and need regular attention.

Often, it is better to combine two pumps in the pond – one to run the filtration and another to run any ornaments or fountains separately. This means that, if you are away from home, the filtration will keep running even if the fountain clogs and slows down.

One advantage of submersible pumps is that any excess heat the pump produces will be transferred to the water, acting as a small heater in winter.

EXTERNAL PUMPS

External pumps are ideal where access to the inlet of the pond is difficult. An inlet screen will be required to stop fish from being sucked up the pipe.

External pumps generally use more electricity than submersible types (see above) and most are based around a swimming pool pump design. As they suck water from the pond, they require heavy-duty, flexible hose or glued, rigid pipework. This can be difficult to install and is prone to frost damage if not protected well.

External pumps do not transfer heat to the water, so they waste more energy than submersibles. However, they are often better for larger pond systems as they are available in larger sizes. Maintenance is easier, too, due to the dry installation and the fact that most are fitted with a large pre-filter basket.

SHOPPING LIST
- *Pump*
- *Good-quality pipework (the largest the pump will accept)*
- *Stainless steel pipe clips*
- *Screwdriver (for clips)*
- *Extra fittings for pipework – elbows, tees, valves, etc.*

> *Tip: Always use the largest pipework possible for any particular model of pump, as the flow rate the manufacturer lists will assume use of the largest pipework.*

CALCULATING FLOW RATE
The following graph is an example of how to work out the flow rate at a given head.

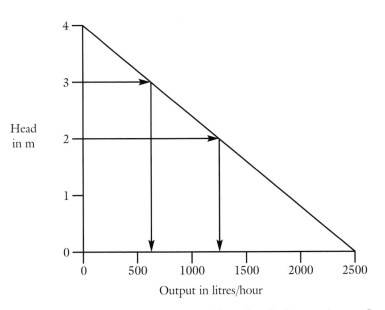

This shows that, at a 2-metre (6-feet) head, the maximum flow rate would be 1,250 litres (275 UK gallons or 330 US fluid gallons) per hour (indicated by black arrows). Remember, this is maximum value; it does not take into account hose diameter, length, in-line ultraviolet filters, and spray bars, so add extra height for each item.

The head of water the pump has to work against is the distance from the water surface of the pond (the depth of the pond does not make much difference) to the highest point to which the water is pumped and discharged. The head has to include factors covering the following extras:

- The size of your pond will affect the size of filter you require, and this will dictate the flow rate you need.
- Size of pipework. More energy is needed to pump water through a narrow pipe, so use the maximum pipe size the pump can take.
- The number of turns and fittings within the pipework will also have an effect. For example, a 90-degree elbow produces the same resistance as pumping up a 0.1-metre (8-inch) head.
- Ultraviolet filters are, on average, equivalent to a 0.2-metre (16-inch) head.
- A spray bar in a filter box is the same as a 0.2-metre (16-inch) head.

PIPE RECOMMENDATIONS

- *Use minimum 20-mm (0.8-inch) pipework for pumps up to 1,800 litres/hour (396 UK gallons or 476 US fluid gallons per hour). A 5-metre (16-feet, 4-inch) length of 20-mm (0.8-inch) pipe is equal to a 0.5-metre (20-inch) head loss.*
- *Use 25-mm pipework for pumps up to 3,000 litres/hour (660 UK gallons or 793 US fluid gallons per hour). A 5-metre (16-feet, 4-inch) length of 25-mm (1-inch) pipe is equal to a 1-metre (40-inch) head loss.*
- *Use 32-mm (1.2-inch) pipework for pumps up to 4,500 litres/hour (990 UK gallons or 1189 US fluid gallons per hour). A 5-metre (16-feet, 4-inch) length of 32-mm (1.2-inch) pipe is equal to a 0.25-metre (10-inch) head loss.*
- *Use 38- to 40-mm (1.5-inch) pipework for pumps up to 15,000 litres/hour (3,300 UK gallons or 3,963 US fluid gallons per hour). A 5-metre (16-feet, 4-inch) length of 38- to 40-mm (1.5-inch) pipe is equal to a 0.75-metre (30-inch) head loss.*

Note: While these figures may seem odd, the faster you pump the water through a pipe, the more resistance it will encounter. Hence, the newer, solid handling pumps work well with large pipework only, as it offers little resistance to these low-power motors.

AN EXAMPLE

Here is an example of how these extras could affect a pump's output.

A small pond has a 1.9-metre-high (6 feet) waterfall, 5 metres of 20-mm (0.8-inch) pipe, two 90-degree elbows, an ultraviolet filter, and a box filter with spray bar.

The total head would be 1.9 metres (6 feet) + 0.5 metres (3 feet) + 0.2 metres (8 inches) or 2 x 0.1 metres (2 x 4 inches) + 0.2 metres (8 inches) + 0.2 metres (8 inches) = a 3-metre (approximately a 10-feet) head. On the pump chart (indicated by red arrows), this would leave a flow rate of only 600 litres per hour (132 UK gallons or 159 US fluid gallons), far too low for all but the smallest pond. A larger pump would be needed. Some pumps will not be affected as much by higher heads, but these consume more electricity and so cost more to run.

CHOOSING YOUR PUMP

When you have decided on the flow rate needed, you can purchase your pump. Consider the following factors and see which best fits your application.

- Is the pump going to run 24 hours a day, 7 days a week, or just for short periods? Running costs will be important if it is going to run all the time. If it will only run for short periods, you can afford to install one that is more greedy with electricity.
- Is the pump to run a fountain/ornament or a filter, or both? A filter-only pump can pump solids and waste, whereas a fountain pump needs a pre-filter to prevent the fountain head from clogging.
- Is getting to the pump for maintenance easy or difficult? If access to the pump in the pond is difficult, it may be advisable to go for an external pump.

When comparing pumps, there are other factors to consider as well as running costs and purchase price.

- Warranty. A short warranty means the manufacturer expects the pump to last a short time! Some warranties exclude wearing parts.
- Are spares readily available? Some manufacturers do not supply spares, except the most basic (such as filter foams). This may

seem irrelevant, but, if you break the impeller and you can't buy a spare, the pump will be scrap.

• Low voltage or mains power? The best pumps tend to be mains, as the transformers for larger pumps are very expensive. However, if there is a chance that young children could gain access to the pump, then low voltage should be considered.

If in doubt, ask your retailer for advice. If you can, take a photograph or drawing of your pond so that he or she can see exactly what you are talking about. Before leaving the shop, check the pump for damage or missing parts. Get the retailer to go through the cleaning process with you, and show you all the parts and how to assemble them. If the pump has a foam pre-filter, buy a spare. You will need it.

INSTALLING YOUR PUMP

Read the instructions carefully *before* you have a problem, rather than after something has gone wrong. For example, are there any special requirements for the pump? Is there packaging inside the pump that needs to be removed?

Once the pump is unpacked, connect the hose with a stainless steel hose clip. Do not use mild steel as it will rust, and you will not be able to remove it. Galvanised clips are not suitable, as some pond chemicals react with the zinc in the clip, which could poison the fish.

Once the clip is in place, wrap it with an offcut of pond liner. This will stop the fish damaging themselves by rubbing against it. It will also prevent the clip from damaging the liner if the pump should fall over.

Place the pump in the pond and run the cable to the electrical supply. If it is to be hard wired (i.e. not a plug and socket), make sure the pump has a fuse and a residual circuit breaker (RCB) to protect you and your fish from faults. If you are unsure of the wiring get an electrician to fit it.

All electrical sockets should be placed at least 2 metres (6.5 feet) away from the water so that it is not possible to touch the supply and the water at the same time. There must be a switch nearby so that the pump can be isolated when maintenance is carried out.

With the pump underwater, or, in the case of an external pump, with the pipework full of water, check that all valves are open and the pipes are not kinked, and then switch on the pump. It should start to work, but, if not, turn it off and check all wiring and valves. *Never put your hands into the water with a pump that is connected to the supply.* When you are satisfied that you have checked everything, turn on the electrical supply once again. If the pump still does not work, take it back to the shop and ask the retailer to check it, as dismantling it yourself may invalidate the warranty.

PUMP MAINTENANCE

The most regularly asked question about a pump is 'How often will it need cleaning?' The only honest answer to this is 'Every pond is different. You will soon find out.' As the pump clogs, it will slow down, and you will know it needs cleaning.

Basic maintenance is the same for all pumps. Clean the pre-filter and check the impeller for trapped solids. If the pump is not cleaned, it will either overheat or the impeller will stop moving and break. If you want the pump to last, maintenance is the key. New pond pump cleaning products are now available from your retailer.

CLEANING A SUBMERSIBLE PUMP

- Turn off the pump at the electrical supply before removing it from the water or disconnecting any pipework.
- Wash the pump and remove any algae or mud from the casing. Algae growth can cause overheating and mud can enter the bearings when you take it apart to clean.
- Don't take the pump apart over the pond, as small parts may fall into the water.
- Remove the pre-filter and impeller housing (if possible) and wash well.
- Take out the impeller, if possible, but be careful not to break the shaft. Wash it in water. Clean inside the motor housing.
- Use the reverse procedure to re-assemble the pump, being careful not to get dirt on the impeller shaft or any 'o'-rings that are present.

CLEANING AN EXTERNAL PUMP

- Turn off the electrical supply. Close off valves to and from the pump to stop water rushing out over the pump.

- Remove the pre-filter from the pond and clean it.
- Remove the pre-filter basket on the pump (if there is one), and wash out.
- Unless the impeller is visibly jammed, do not take the pump apart to check, unless you suspect there is a blockage.
- To start up, reverse the above steps.

The frequency of this will vary from pump to pump, and from pond to pond, but check the pump at least once a month. If the pump jams and the motor cannot turn, it will overheat and either melt or short-circuit. Although many pumps have thermo cut-outs, they are not designed to be left for long periods without cleaning or maintenance.

CHAPTER 6

FILTRATION

> 1. Mechanical filtration
> 2. Biological filtration
> 3. Ready-made filters
> 4. Ultraviolet systems

A filter system serves two purposes in a pond. The first is to act as a mechanical filter and the second as a biological filter. Not all ponds need filters, but, in most cases where fish are the priority, they will be required to keep the water clear and toxic levels under control.

What works for one pond may not work for another, so seek advice from a reputable supplier. Do not buy the smallest and cheapest filter you can find – look around for the best product that will be easy to maintain and can run for a reasonable amount of time between cleaning.

> *Tip: Small, compact filters will clog quickly as they have less media than larger ones and will require more maintenance.*

MECHANICAL FILTRATION
The purpose of mechanical filtration is to remove particles from suspension and so reduce the load on the biological section of the

filter. It is the most important stage to get right for a number of reasons:

- If large quantities of waste get through to the biological section of the filter, it will clog the filter media and reduce the filter's capacity to break down waste products.
- The more organic waste there is, the more oxygen is required to break it down. More oxygen demand means less for the fish in times of hardship, such as in hot weather.
- The quicker the large waste matter is removed, the less work the biological filter has to do, and the lower the nitrate level will be. This means less food for the algae, and less algae growth.
- If waste is kept to a minimum, the size of the biological filter can be smaller, as it will have less work to do.

There are a number of methods of mechanical filtration, the most common using a screen or media to remove or trap particles. The basic principle of the settlement tank is to slow the water flow so that the suspended particles fall to the base of the tank, from where they can be removed with ease.

In order to break up and slow the flow of water, a number of types of media have been created.

FILTER BRUSH

This is the most common, yet it is often used incorrectly. The brush should hang in the flow so that the water has to pass through the side, not from beneath through the brush's end.

The water level should be below the top of the brush to stop the water by-passing the settlement system by flowing over the top of it.

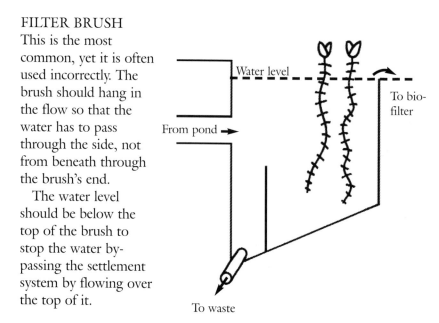

Water level

From pond →

To bio-filter

To waste

The brush system's biggest drawback is cleaning, which is messy and time-consuming.

BIO BLOCK

This is another medium that is now available, created by joining net tubes into 'blocks' that can be used in the filter either whole or cut to fit. This medium has many advantages over the others, the most important being easy maintenance and the fact that it is almost impossible to clog. Flow rates are 7,500 to 10,000 litres per hour per square metre of surface area (1,650 to 2,200 UK gallons or 1,981 to 2,642 US fluid gallons per hour per square yard). The longer it is established, the better it works, as the bacteria build up a filter web between the net elements and trap the finer particles.

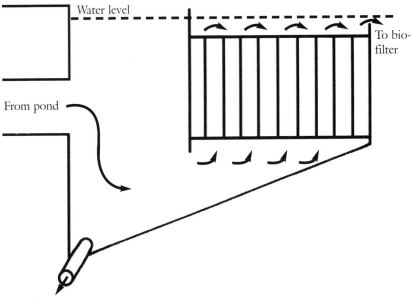

VORTEX

The vortex is seldom used properly because many that are sold are poorly designed. The flow rate is vital. Water enters the vortex at a 90-degree tangent to the side. This causes the water to spin, creating a vortex (see picture overleaf for basic design).

At the correct flow, the waste works its way to the centre of the tank and falls into a collecting chamber. If the flow is too fast, the vortex will pick up the waste (like a tornado) and carry it on to the next stage of filtration.

The exit of the vortex can also affect the efficiency of the unit. There are two types of exit. One is a centrally mounted pipe that is set just below the water level and collects the water from the middle of the water column (A). The other is an outer trough that collects the surface water as it overflows from around the edge (B).

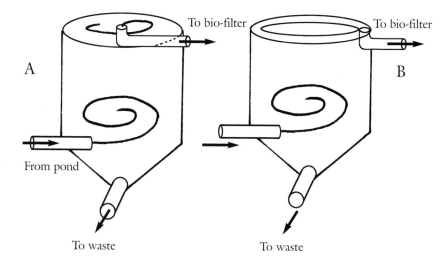

The ideal flow rate is between 12,000 to 17,500 litres per hour per square metre (2,640 to 3,850 UK gallons or 3,170 to 4,623 US fluid gallons per hour per square yard) of surface area for tanks more than 1 metre (3 feet, 3 inches) deep. Generally, shallower tanks do not work very well unless the flow rate is slowed right down to suit. This tends to make them redundant, as brushes work better.

EXAMPLE
If a vortex tank is 0.9 metres (35 inches) in diameter, the surface area will be 0.9 x 0.9, which is equal to 0.81 square metres (or 35 x 35 inches, which is equal to 8.5 square feet). Therefore, the average flow required would be 0.81 x 15,000 (15,000 litres being the ideal flow rate

per square metre) or 8.5 x 3,300 (UK imperial) or 8.5 x 4010 (US imperial), which is equal to 12,100 litres (2,665 UK gallons or 3,235 US fluid gallons) per hour. As with any system, the flow rate will differ from one pond set-up to another, so some amount of trial and error will be needed to get the best results.

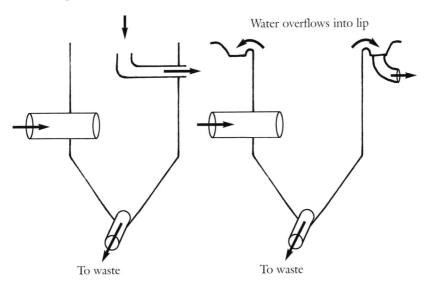

Water overflows into lip

To waste   To waste

BAFFLE TANKS

An older system that works very well, requires very little maintenance, but needs a large tank as the flow rates are very slow. The baffles are set at angles from the vertical plain of 32.5 degrees to 45 degrees, depending on the flow rate. As the water enters the tank, it works its way up to the surface, depositing waste particles along the way. If you have the space this is a very good system, but is difficult to set up and get started.

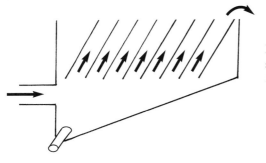

Baffle plates
set between
32.5° and 45°

PRESSURISED SAND FILTERS

These were designed to remove low volumes of small particles in relatively clean environments, so the garden pond is not an ideal situation for them. They are expensive to purchase and run, as they require a large pump with a high-pressure rating to clean them. They require regular cleaning as they clog very quickly and in some situations can cause gas bubble disease in fish (see chapter twelve).

The principle of the filter is to force the dirty water through a sand bed and, as the water passes through, the particles are left behind. The more the filter clogs, the better it works, but the flow rate slows down as well. The filter is controlled by a multi-port valve that allows easy selection from a variety of settings – normal filtration, backwashing for cleaning, rinse to stop waste entering the pond, and recirculation. This allows work to be carried out to the filter without stopping the pump, although it is always recommended that you switch the pump off while working with water.

The backwash cycle requires a large pump, typically a 1hp, to backwash a 60-cm (2-feet) filter. There is 100 kg (220 lbs) of sand to lift in a 60-cm (2-feet) filter during the backwash process, as the clean water is forced to the bottom of the filter and then up through the sand and out to waste.

HIGH RATE SAND FILTER

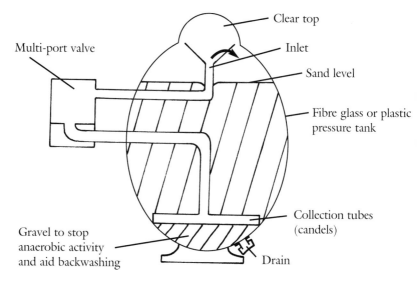

Multi-port valve

Clear top

Inlet

Sand level

Fibre glass or plastic pressure tank

Collection tubes (candels)

Gravel to stop anaerobic activity and aid backwashing

Drain

DRUM FILTER

The drum filter is the best method of particle removal, in my experience. It is the choice of the fish farmer, and these are the advantages:

- Drum filters can filter down to 20 microns with ease. At this level, they can remove algae that cause green water, free-swimming parasites and almost all waste particles, leaving clear water to pass to the biological filter.
- Once dirty, they clean themselves. The waste is washed away, so there is nothing is left to do.
- The efficiency of these units means they can be very small, and, therefore, they don't waste space.
- The quick removal of waste means the nitrate levels remain lower for longer and fewer water changes are needed.

The main drawback to the drum filter is cost, which meant they have mainly been the preserve of the fish farmer. However, a new version, called a screen filter, has recently been developed at a much lower price. Ask your supplier for details.

PRESSURE FILTER

The pressure filter was hailed as the answer when it came on the market because it solved so many problems that pondkeepers had had to put up with when using other pump-fed filters.
It enables the filter to be positioned below water level, which makes it easy to hide and install. The simple set-up and design has made the pressure filter very popular, but there are several things you need to bear in mind to get the best from it.

1) The pressure filter is pressurised, as the name suggests, which means it will put back pressure on the pump. A small, low-pressure pump therefore will not be able to run it once the filter starts to get dirty, and the pressure requirement increases. It will be unable to force water through the filter.

2) The filter is difficult to clean, as it has to be taken apart to clean the foams (the backwash facility offered does not work very well). The unit then has to be watertight when closed up again, and many of the units on the market are very difficult to reseal. I suggest you have a go at this before buying the unit.

3) The flow rate through the filter will slow as it clogs with waste and this can put the fish at risk during warm weather as no water movement can mean no oxygen supply. There is no by-pass should the filter media clog.

4) Maintenance must be carried out on a regular basis to ensure a good flow. If the filter is allowed to clog, the pump will burn out without water flowing through it to cool and lubricate it.

> *Tip: If you decide this style of filter is for you then always have a back-up pump just in case the filter clogs.*

BIOLOGICAL FILTRATION
After the removal of solid waste, the next stage is the reduction of dissolved waste, such as ammonia and nitrite. The biological filter is an area devoted to the support and concentration of bacteria needed to break down the waste.

THE NITROGEN CYCLE

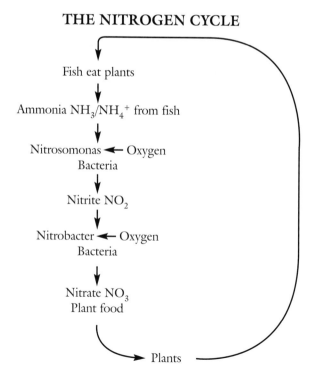

Fish eat plants

Ammonia NH_3/NH_4^+ from fish

Nitrosomonas ← Oxygen
Bacteria

Nitrite NO_2

Nitrobacter ← Oxygen
Bacteria

Nitrate NO_3
Plant food

Plants

The waste from the fish is the start of the nitrogen cycle, shown here in simplified form.

When fish are fed, they convert food into body mass and use some as energy to live. The waste is excreted in the form of ammonia. Nitrosomonas, the naturally occurring bacteria in the pond, break ammonia down to nitrite, using oxygen. Once this has been done, the next set of bacteria, nitrobacters, get to work converting nitrite to nitrate. This process also requires oxygen.

The final product, nitrate, is plant food. Pond plants good and bad (algae) need this to grow, and will consume as much as they can. However, the nitrate level will usually rise, as it is unlikely that the plants in the pond will be able to keep up with the nitrate produced.

The bacteria have a few simple requirements, the first being oxygen, which is needed to break down ammonia to nitrite and nitrite to nitrate.

The food required is readily supplied by the fish, in the form of ammonia.

The important issues that affect biological filters are:

- **Oxygen supply:** Without oxygen, the bacteria will die and anaerobic bacteria will take over, converting nitrate back to nitrite, which poisons the fish. The oxygen level needs to be as high as possible. The addition of air stones to the filter will help the process.
- **Temperature:** The higher the temperature, the better the filter will work, until the oxygen level drops off at very high temperatures.
- **Chemicals in the water:** Many treatments will affect the filter's efficiency either by reducing the oxygen levels or by directly killing the bacteria.
- **Water flow:** As the water brings both the food and oxygen, this is a very important factor. A good flow rate to aim for is 8 to 10 times the volume of the bio-filter per hour. The filter will work at much higher speeds, but this is the ideal rate.

FILTER MEDIA

The filter medium is the bacteria's home and should offer a large surface area, as the more bacteria it supports, the more work the filter can do. The medium needs to be rough so that the bacteria can grow on the surface. It must have a good structure, so that water flows evenly through it, otherwise 'dead' areas can become anaerobic (oxygen deficient).

There is a range of filter media on the market, ranging from lava rock to plastic sheeting. Each needs to fulfil the following basic requirements:

- It should be non-toxic and contain no recycled material. It is difficult to confirm the content of a recycled product.
- It should have a large surface-to-volume ratio. The more bacteria the media can hold, the smaller the filter can be.
- It should contain no glue, as this will eventually fail and pollute the water.
- It must be easy to clean. This is very important if the efficiency is to be high, as dirty filters consume more oxygen and do less work.
- The medium must not clog. If it does, it will turn anaerobic and convert nitrate back to nitrite.
- It must be easy to handle and install. This is often a considerable problem with media that have small components, as it can be difficult to hold them in place or support them.
- It should not compact or lock itself together, otherwise cleaning is impossible. Most of the 'aqua rocks' sold compact with time and are very difficult to clean properly. The compacting medium also creates tracking, where the water only runs through in areas of the least restriction. This effectively stops part of the medium working and reduces the amount of work that the filter can do. Tracking also increases the likelihood of the filter blocking, and the production of anaerobic areas.
- Weight is also a key factor, as it affects the tank required for the filter. Gravel weighs about 1500 kg per cubic metre (about 3,300 lbs per cubic yard), and this will have to be taken into account when building and installing the tank. This will also affect the cost. The medium might be cheaper, but, if the tank is more expensive, a lightweight medium may be a better bet.
- The medium must have a known surface area-to-volume ratio, so that you can work out the filter size.

GRAVEL
Gravel is cheap, but fulfils few of the criteria listed above. It compacts, is difficult to clean, and is very heavy.

AQUA ROCK

Aqua rock is either crushed lava rock or clinker (the waste from kilns). It is very difficult to clean and has a poor surface area-to-volume ratio.

LYTAG

This is an expanded clay pellet that has a large, porous surface area and often floats. It can be difficult to clean and clogs easily.

FLOCOR

Flocor is a plastic medium created for sewage farms. It has a very good surface area-to-volume ratio and is relatively inexpensive. It is used extensively on commercial fish farms. Its ultralight weight makes filter construction simple and it is easy to handle. The only downside is that, as a loose medium, it traps dirt and is quite difficult to clean.

JAPANESE FILTER MAT

This is a jumble of plastic fibres bonded together, and is highly thought of by some fish retailers and koi experts. However, I don't recommend it. It is glued together, and the glue eventually fails, leaving small plastic fibres floating around the filters and finding their way to the pump, which they then clog. It has a random construction and no set surface area-to-volume ratio. The mat is a mix of different plastics, and no data is available on the make-up of it. The mat needs to be cut up and turned into cartridges, otherwise it clogs quickly. It is difficult to clean.

BIO BLOCK

Bio Block is a very good medium, easy to clean and with a large surface area-to-volume ratio. Its open structure is not prone to clogging and offers an even flow path for the water, and therefore no tracking. It is strong and easy to install as it in comes in blocks that can be cut to fit the tank. Very popular with commercial farms due to its high surface area-to-cost ratio. Can be used for settlement and biological sections of the filter.

PLASTIC

Plastic is available in many forms, but most have problems when it comes to the surface. It is cheaper to produce a medium with a smooth surface, so most manufacturers do. This leaves the bacteria with nothing to cling to. This type of medium will take a very long time to mature, and, if the water flow is too strong, the bacteria will be washed off.

BIO BALLS

Bio balls were one of the first effective plastic media, but they can be used only in a filter where the first stages remove all the solids, as they clog quite quickly and are difficult to clean. They offer a very large surface area, but the complex nature of the design makes them difficult to produce, and this is reflected in the high production cost. They are best used in trickle towers.

BIO GLASS

Bio glass is a very expensive medium, as it is a honeycomb of glass made into small sections in the shape of a doughnut. The surface area is incredibly large – about 100 times the area of most other media. However, it has never proved totally satisfactory in ponds due to the high particle waste levels in the water. The surface of the medium is so fine it clogs almost immediately and is of little use after a few weeks. It is ideally suited for indoor tanks.

READY-MADE FILTERS

The simplest filters consist of a foam pre-filter on the front of the pump. These work in small ponds up to 500 litres (110 UK gallons or 132 US fluid gallons), but require regular maintenance and, if left too long, will starve the pump of water and cause it to fail. They are not really suitable for ponds containing lots of fish, due to the relatively poor filter capacity and high maintenance.

The next step up is a plastic water tank with a spray bar spreading the water across thin sheets of foam of varying grades. This collects the particles and any dirt in the water. A plastic ring, which offers a large surface area-to-volume ratio, is used for bacteria to live on for the biological action to take place.

You can also buy a multi-chamber filter (see opposite). In this type of filter the different filtration stages are split up, which allows the use of more media and means the biological media are left undisturbed during cleaning.

FOAM FILTER

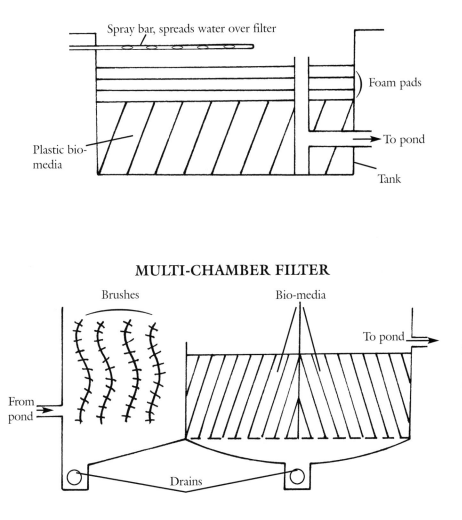

MULTI-CHAMBER FILTER

For example, a simple three-chamber model uses brushes in the first chamber for settlement and then has two biological chambers for the bacteria. This offers the chance of using two different media, which means diverse habitats for the bacteria to grow in and improves the filter's efficiency. There is a perforated tray to hold up the medium and allow the water to flow underneath to the next chamber. The settlement chamber has a drain to waste for easy maintenance.

Multiple vortex filters are a newer design, popular with manufacturers as they are cheaper to produce and stronger than 'box'-shaped filters. They come in three, four or five-chamber styles and the medium choice is up to you. The vortices are normally very small and the flow rates recommended are far too quick. To get the best from these filters you need to buy a larger size than most manufacturers suggest and slow down the flow rate. All chambers have drains, making cleaning easy and quick. They are best used as gravity-fed filters, otherwise the pump breaks up the solids, making collection more difficult.

FLUIDISED FILTER BEDS

These are biological only and require a good pre-filter to prevent solids from entering the system. They are very effective and very compact for their capacity, but they have particular requirements:

MOVING BED FILTER

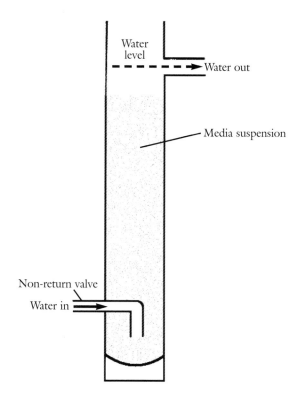

- They need a high capacity pump to start and lift the media into suspension.
- The flow rate must be constant. Any large variation will stop the filter from functioning. If it is too high, the media will end up in the pond; too low, and they will settle out and turn anaerobic.
- They require well-oxygenated water to function, as a vast amount of bacteria is held in a very small area.
- The filter must be vertical to work correctly, otherwise the media will settle out on one side, creating an anaerobic section.
- They must never be used without a normal biological filter as they are, by nature, unreliable and should be considered as an additional filter, rather than the main one.
- They are affected by chemicals and die quickly if the water flow stops as the media stops moving, sinks to the bottom and compacts down, leaving the bacteria without oxygen.

Fluidised filters are normally only for marine systems and commercial indoor recirculation systems. They should be made of stainless steel or a tough industrial plastic, as the moving sand particles will soon wear out thin plastic or fibre glass tanks.

TRICKLE TOWERS

In the commercial world, these are the most popular as they offer the best of all filter methods, though it is only biological.

The medium is suspended in air, which has an oxygen content about 20 times higher than in water and can, therefore, support 20 times the bacteria of a traditional submerged filter. The action of water falling down the medium exposes it to the air, helping to remove ammonia which is lost to the atmosphere. This reduces the work the filter has to do, and, at the same time, it reduces nitrate, so reducing algae growth.

The design is simple and reliable. It has few special requirements and so is easy to set up and run. The tower can be lightweight as it holds no water and only has to hold the filter medium upright and contain any water as it falls through. It is even possible to use thin plastic sheeting as a tower if the medium will self-support. This reduces the initial outlay. The spray bar needs to spread the water evenly over the surface of the medium, which is best achieved with a rotating bar.

The filter needs to be at least 1.2 metres (4 feet) high to be effective. Its efficiency can be improved as the fish increase in size by simply adding an air pump to the filter base, so that air is allowed to work its way up the filter and out of the top. This increases the oxygen levels and removes any ammonia that is forced out of the water. Another easy way to increase the flow of air is to add an extractor fan to the tower to pull air through the medium.

The two drawbacks of trickle towers are height – they need to be tall to work, and they have to be above the water level of the pond – and temperature. As they pass water through the air, energy will be exchanged between the two elements. In warm weather, they will heat the water; in cold weather, they will cool it. If power is lost, they can survive undamaged for days without much loss of efficiency, as the air in the tower is humid and full of oxygen.

BEAD FILTERS

Bead filters are not new, but have become available to the pondkeeper only in recent times. They are based on the simple principle of using small, floating plastic beads, about 3 to 4 mm (0.15 inches) in diameter, to act as both a mechanical and biological filter. The design makes them very compact and easy to hide. They are also easy to clean, as a simple timer that switches the pump off for 15 minutes a day will start its cleaning cycle. A good pre-filter is needed to remove any trace of blanket weed or particles larger than 5 mm (0.2 inches) as these will clog the inlet strainer and reduce the throughput of water.

The hour-glass shape has become the trademark of the best models, as they clean themselves without the use of any moving parts and have proved to be very reliable.

Bead filters are slow to start working and seem to suffer if chemicals are added to the pond, but, once established, they are very good. Use units that are larger than recommended as they are inclined to underperform some manufacturers' figures. They are ideal if time is limited and you are away from home regularly, as the self-cleaning makes maintenance very simple.

SETTING UP A BIOLOGICAL FILTER

All biological filters take time to process waste as bacteria need to build up to sufficient numbers before the filter begins working

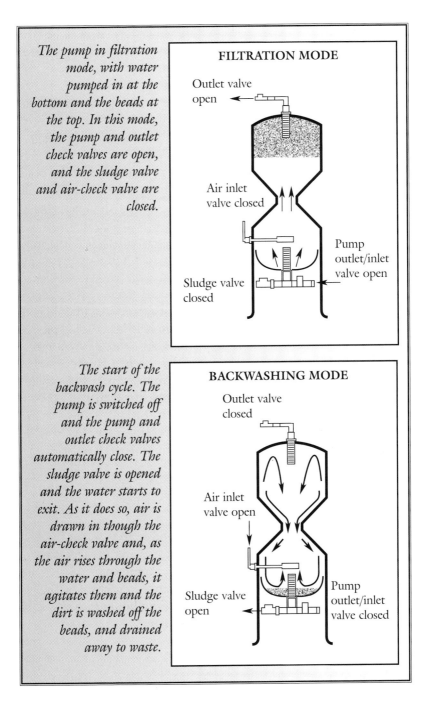

The pump in filtration mode, with water pumped in at the bottom and the beads at the top. In this mode, the pump and outlet check valves are open, and the sludge valve and air-check valve are closed.

FILTRATION MODE

Outlet valve open

Air inlet valve closed

Pump outlet/inlet valve open

Sludge valve closed

The start of the backwash cycle. The pump is switched off and the pump and outlet check valves automatically close. The sludge valve is opened and the water starts to exit. As it does so, air is drawn in though the air-check valve and, as the air rises through the water and beads, it agitates them and the dirt is washed off the beads, and drained away to waste.

BACKWASHING MODE

Outlet valve closed

Air inlet valve open

Sludge valve open

Pump outlet/inlet valve closed

Once the tank is drained, the beads are in the expansion chamber at the base of the tank, clean and dirt-free. The sludge valve can now be closed and the pump switched on. The filter then refills, the air-check valve closes and the outlet valve opens.

The beads start to rise to the top to begin working again.

NOTE: The sludge valve can be replaced with an automatic valve that opens as soon as the pump is switched off. This means the filter unit can be left to self-clean and restart.

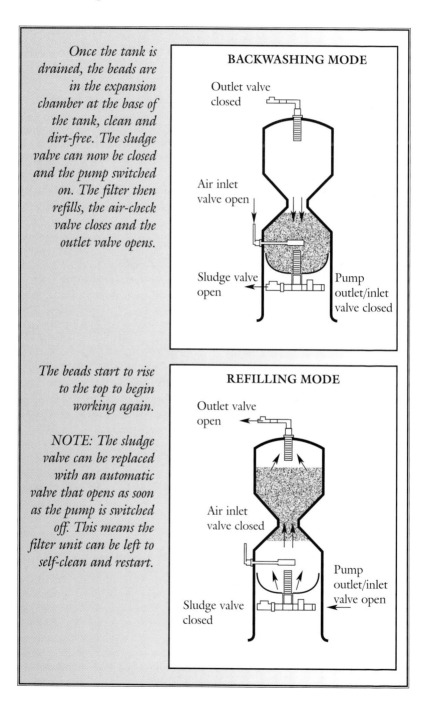

BACKWASHING MODE

Outlet valve closed

Air inlet valve open

Sludge valve open

Pump outlet/inlet valve closed

REFILLING MODE

Outlet valve open

Air inlet valve closed

Sludge valve closed

Pump outlet/inlet valve open

efficiently. The build-up time can be reduced by adding a bacterial filter start. This contains all the nitrifying bacteria in a solution that suspends them in an inactive mode. As soon as they are added to water, the bacteria start to function and multiply. At this point all ultraviolet filters should be left off to avoid a sterilising effect.

Some ponds can experience 'new pond syndrome', in which the addition of excess fish leads to the death of most of them. This is caused by the immature filter not being able to break down the fish waste.

When starting a new pond, it should not be stocked heavily for at least four to six weeks to avoid this effect and fish should be added in small numbers after first being quarantined. Testing the water in a new pond will help you to determine when it is safe to add new fish as the start-up of the filter follows a simple path.

As the first fish are added, waste is produced as ammonia. This shows on a test kit and the level rises over time until the bacteria appear in sufficient numbers to convert it to nitrite. The nitrite will start to rise as the ammonia is converted and will continue until the bacteria that convert nitrite to nitrate reach the correct numbers and the level then drops. The nitrate level rises until it is either expelled by water changing, or used by plants.

The speed at which the filter starts is affected by water temperature and available oxygen. The higher the temperature and oxygen content, the faster the filter will establish itself.

FILTER START-UP CYCLE

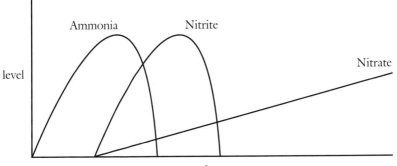

> *Tip: Every time you add fish to the pond, the filter has to build up more bacteria to help with the increased load. Often, this is called shock loading and many filters, especially small filters that are on the limit of their capacity, fail, and a complete breakdown leads to instantaneous waste build-up and fish deaths. So, when adding a number of fish to your pond, always check the levels for a few days to make sure this does not occur.*

SIZING THE FILTER

The creation of a biological filter is very simple, but sizing can be difficult as ideas range from one-third the size of the pond to a tiny 25-litre (5.5-UK-gallon or 6.6-US-fluid-gallon) tank.

I suggest you allow 1 litre of filter media for each gram of food per day (or 0.2 UK/US gallons per oz of food). A fish requires 2 per cent of its body weight per day to live a healthy life with normal growth. So, if your pond is to hold say 10 fish at 60 cm (2 feet) in length, a fish this size would weigh about 3 kgs (6.6 lbs). A feed weight of 3000 x 2 per cent = 60 g x 10 = 600 g of food per day so a biological filter holding 600 litres of media will be fine. Alternatively, provide 20 oz of food per 133 UK gallons or 160 US gallons.

It is always best to oversize your filter as this formula works well when the temperature is constant, which it seldom is. Allow 10 to 15 per cent extra in the filter media to cover any variations or extra fish. When building a filter, allow some extra space around it for extensions later.

NITRATE FILTERS

The last process of the aerobic filter is the production of nitrate. Although it is not toxic until levels are very high – in excess of 150 mg per litre – the lower the levels, the better for the fish. In the fishes' natural habitat, nitrate would be less than 1 mg per litre (see chapter nine).

There are three ways to remove nitrate effectively – with a filter, with plants, or with ion-exchange resin.

DENITRIFING FILTERS

A simple denitrifing filter is a one that supports bacteria that require oxygen-free conditions.

Denitrification requires a source of carbon. The normal approach to this is to add either methanol or sugar. The bacteria then break down the carbon source and nitrate to produce carbon dioxide, nitrogen gas and water.

DENTRIFICATION

$$CH_3O_2 + NO_3 \longrightarrow CO_3 + N_2 + H_2O$$

(Methanol)   Nitrate   Nitrogen gas   Water

Nitrite is reduced to Nitrate before conversion to Nitrogen gas.

However, setting up and maintaining a denitrifying filter tank is quite complex, time-consuming and carries some risk to fish if it goes wrong. I would not recommend it to inexperienced fishkeepers.

PLANTS

The most natural way to remove nitrate from the pond is to use plants. As plants grow, they use nitrate to build the stems and leaves, which collect sunlight to produce food for further growth. Also, as they grow, they require more nitrogen. The more the plants are cut and removed, the more they grow, which means they will remove more nitrate. The plants also pick up other toxic metals and chemicals, so they are good for purifying the water as well.

NITRATE REMOVAL

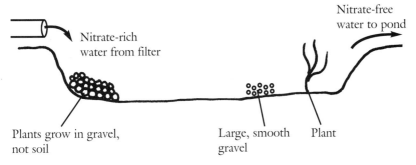

Nitrate-rich water from filter

Nitrate-free water to pond

Plants grow in gravel, not soil

Large, smooth gravel

Plant

The best way to grow plants for a vegetable filter is to house them in a shallow water course fed from the biological filter, where nitrate production occurs.

The simpler the filter design, the better it works, as the maintenance is also simple. The vegetable filter should be large enough for the flow from the bio filter, and long, so that the water takes a reasonable time to travel through the filter and the plants have a chance to pick up the nitrate as it goes past in the water. The plants will need regular trimming to ensure maximum growth. The only downside is that plants do not grow well in the winter months when the weather is cold.

ION-EXCHANGE RESIN

You can use resins that remove nitrate in exchange for another ion, usually sodium chloride (common salt). The resin is 'cleaned' or recharged by washing in a salt solution of 100 g per litre of water (3.5 oz per 0.2 UK gallons/US fluid gallons). Each litre (0.2 UK gallons/US fluid gallons) of resin needs 5 litres (1 UK gallon or 1.4 US fluid gallons) of salt solution to recharge it. This is the easiest method for removal if the space for a vegetable filter is not available.

Resins are compact and very good. As a rough guide, you will need approximately 1 litre (0.2 UK/US fluid gallons) of resin for each 5,000 litres (1,099 UK gallons or 1,320 US fluid gallons) of pond volume.

ULTRAVIOLET SYSTEMS

These are probably the least understood pond products on the market. They are sold to cure every problem from blanket weed to parasite infestations, but in fact, the standard pond unit cures one pond condition only – green water.

This is done by passing the green water through a bath of UV light, which effectively prevents the algae from reproducing. The water then clears and all is well, as long as the bulb lasts. However, the pond water will go green again if the pond plants have not grown enough to compete with the algae.

All UV systems work by circulating pond water around a UV bulb – whether that is an older, double-ended bulb or a newer, single-ended type – encased within a quartz sleeve to prevent direct contact with the water. The outer case directs the water along the outside of the sleeve, ideally, in a spiral pattern, to allow maximum contact time with the UV light so that no water can escape the rays.

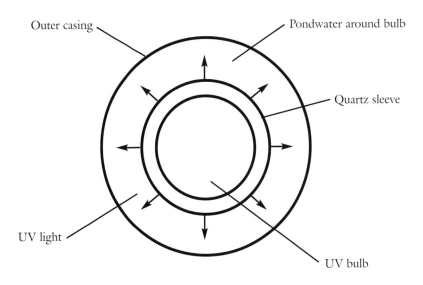

There are two types of ultraviolet systems available – the standard pond Ultraviolet Clarifier (UVC) and the Ultraviolet Steriliser (UVS). UV light is absorbed very quickly, but there are a number of factors that affect the UV's efficiency:

- The speed at which the water flows through the unit. Too fast and the contact time will be too short, too slow and the algae will grow faster than they can be killed.
- Suspended particles in the water. The more debris the water is carrying, the more light will be absorbed and the less work the UVC will do.
- Dirt on the quartz sleeve. If the sleeve is dirty, the light cannot work properly.
- Chemicals in the water. Any dyes that are used as treatments will affect the light's ability to travel through the water.
- Poorly designed UV units. This is the biggest cause of UVC systems not working. A well-designed, sleeved UV bulb will put about 99 per cent of its output into the water, but few units achieve this.

A major difference between the two forms of UV system is the gap between the quartz and the outer casing. The UVC is designed only to kill algae, so the gap is large (up to 4 cm or 1.5 inches) and allows a high water throughput and low resistance to small pumps. The output near the casing is very low, as the water absorbs the UV light, which means the casing material can be thinner than on a UVS.

The gap on a UVS can be as small as 0.5 cm (0.2 inches), and, in most cases, it is between 1 and 1.5 cm (0.4 and 0.5 inches). This means the UV level is very much higher, and, at this dose, even bacteria, viruses and parasites can be killed. It also takes its toll on the casing. Therefore, UVS systems are normally made from industrial plastic materials or stainless steel. The flow rate has to drop to very low volumes, as the contact time required to kill bacteria is far longer than is necessary to kill algae.

A UVS is best fitted after filters – in the return if possible – as they work better if the water is free from floating particles. A UVC will work on either the dirty or clean side of the filter, as the UV dose is less important.

There are a few myths about UV systems in general:

- **They sterilise the pond and lower the fishes' immunity to disease:** This is untrue. It would be impossible to create a sterile environment in the open area of a garden, and UVCs *do not sterilise* at all. A UVS will keep only waterborne diseases under control.
- **UVCs control blanket weed:** This is unlikely, as the blanket weed does not pass through the UV chamber.
- **UVs affect the water chemistry and this can kill the fish:** No tests have proven this and I have never seen anything to even suggest this could happen – one of the main reasons UV units are used to sterilise drinking water is that they do not affect water chemistry.
- **If the bulb is glowing it is still working:** This is also untrue. The reason the manufacturers of the bulbs give you a life for optimum use is because they know how long their bulbs will last! UV light is invisible, so the fact that you can see a glow is entirely irrelevant.

There is no doubt that Ultraviolet filters play an important part in filtering the pond but, if the biological filters are the correct size and the pond is not overstocked, there is no reason why the UV cannot be used for the start of the season and then turned off as the filters start to work.

A FINAL NOTE
There are always differences of opinion when it comes to filtration, and there will always be the pond that survives with no filters at all. Unfortunately, these are few and far between. There is nothing worse than a green pond, and, with modern pumps and filters, there is no need to put up with one.

CHAPTER 7

BOTTOM DRAINS AND LINER CONNECTORS

1. Fitting a bottom drain
2. Fitting a liner connector
3. Surface skimmers

Gravity-fed filtration has become increasingly popular with koi keepers and owners of larger ponds, as it allows filtration pipework and pumps to be situated away from the pond in an easy-to-maintain area.

To facilitate gravity filtration, liner connectors and bottom drains have become necessary to provide exit points for the water from the pond to the filter. Installing these is now very easy as it is possible to purchase units that can be used in either concrete or liner ponds.

While it is tempting to buy the cheapest you can find, it is often a mistake. The cheaper ones are made of fragile, thin plastic and generally use self-tapping screws to fix them in place. Go for the bolt-together units, as they are more reliable and can be taken apart if necessary.

FITTING A BOTTOM DRAIN

When fitting a liner bottom drain, it is important that the drain is securely fixed in position with concrete. If the drain can move about, it will almost certainly break the seal and leak.

BOTTOM DRAINS AND LINER CONNECTORS

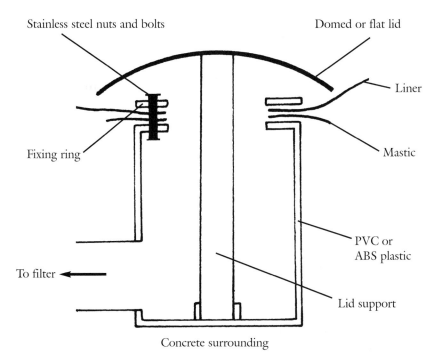

Stainless steel nuts and bolts

Domed or flat lid

Liner

Fixing ring

Mastic

To filter

PVC or ABS plastic

Lid support

Concrete surrounding

With the drain in position, lay the underlay up to, but not over, the drain flange. Next, lay the liner in position, but do not fix the edge of it yet. It is very important to leave enough overlap so that it is possible to move the liner, if need be, once the bottom drain is fixed. Check the liner position again and cut a hole through the liner where the drain is to fit. It should be large enough to fit your hand through. Clean the top of the bottom drain flange and the liner that will be in contact with it, and dry them with a cloth. Apply a generous layer of mastic sealer over the flange using a mastic gun. Then push the liner down in place.

Next, push a pin up through a fixing hole from inside the drain. This will allow you to align the holes without making too many holes in the liner. Align the fixing flange with the pin and drill out the other fixing holes with a sharp drill bit. Insert the stainless steel bolts with a washer. This will stop the bolt head tightening into the plastic flange. When everything is in position, screw on the nut with a washer.

> *Tip: Always use stainless steel nuts and bolts as it will be a nightmare if you have to replace them in a few years' time. If possible, use lock nuts, as they have a plastic insert to stop them becoming loose.*

Tighten the nuts a few turns at a time, to prevent either one of the flanges from cracking or breaking. When this is finished, the liner inside the drain can be trimmed off to the edge of the flange and the excess mastic can be cleaned up at the same time.

When installing bottom drains in concrete ponds it is necessary to sand around the edge of the drain to give the concrete something to bond to. If you are uncertain whether or not the bond will be watertight, it is possible to put a layer of car body filler between the top of the drain and the concrete surface. As body filler will bond to almost anything, it is ideal, and any rough surface can be sanded down to make it level.

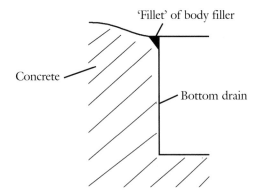

'Fillet' of body filler

Concrete

Bottom drain

FITTING A LINER CONNECTOR
These are fixed to the liner in the same way, but there are a few special points to remember.
- When fixing a liner connector, the liner below it must not be under any pressure, otherwise it will pull out from between the flanges and leak.

• Tightening the nuts and bolts can be problematic with liner connectors, as they will be behind the liner and out of reach. A second pair of hands can hold the nuts in place while the bolts are tightened.

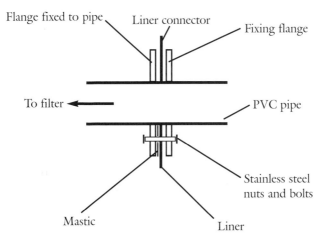

• Holding the pipe in position can also pose a problem, unless you are going to concrete up one side of the pond. An easy way to stop the pipe moving is to dig down the side of the pond and install a paving slab for the pipe to rest on. This will stop it moving down, as it spreads the weight. The pipe can be fixed to the slab with pipe clips, but these will still allow the pipe to move in and out, making fixing much easier.

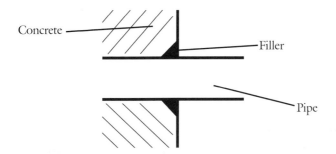

- In concrete ponds, the plain pipe without the flange can be used. Add a layer of car body filler as before with the bottom drain to provide a waterproof seal between the concrete and the plastic pipe.

SURFACE SKIMMERS

Surface skimmers are becoming increasingly popular with koi keepers. They have numerous benefits that should not be overlooked.

- They remove floating debris, such as leaves and dust, which would otherwise sink to the pond base.
- They control floating plants, such as duck weed, as it is easy to collect in a skimmer.
- They constantly remove the surface layer of water and increase the oxygenation of the pond.
- Skimmers remove the oily-looking surface film caused by a build-up of protein from the fish waste. This often forms a white/cream-coloured foam around the base of fountains and waterfalls.

The only possible objection to skimmers is the fact that they will collect food that is on the surface. However, this is far outweighed by their benefits.

TYPES OF SKIMMER

There are two basic designs available for the water gardener – the internal skimmer and the built-in skimmer.

The internal skimmer is a simple but effective unit that stands in the pond and is connected to the inlet of a pump that can handle solids. The water and solids are then pumped to the filter. They are easy to install after the pond has been built and maintenance is simple.

The second type of skimmer is the built-in skimmer. These come in two common styles – the bio skimmer and the swimming pool skimmer – and they are installed as the pond is built.

The bio skimmer was designed especially for ponds. It contains a large basket (this is essential as there is a lot of waste material in a pond) and a solids-handling pump that can be

BIO SKIMMER

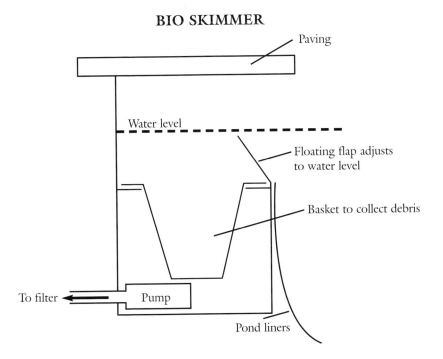

Paving

Water level

Floating flap adjusts to water level

Basket to collect debris

To filter

Pump

Pond liners

connected directly to the filtration unit. This not only saves time and money, but also simplifies the pipework and fitting.

Swimming pool skimmers were the most common variety of skimmer used before the bio came on the market. This skimmer requires a large flow rate to work well, and it has a relatively small basket that clogs quickly, requiring more maintenance. However, it is well built and it will last a long time.

SWIMMING POOL SKIMMER

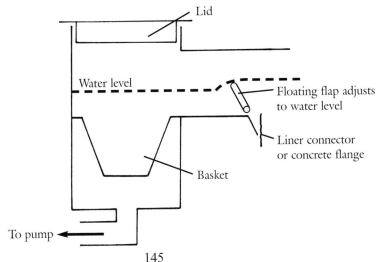

Lid

Water level

Floating flap adjusts to water level

Liner connector or concrete flange

Basket

To pump

INSTALLATION

The installation should be carried out in accordance with the manufacturer's instructions. The liner connectors come with rubber seals, so the use of a mastic sealer is not normally required. The water level should be no more than halfway up the opening to get the best from the skimmer.

The most common mistake when installing a skimmer is the position in the pond. It must be installed at the end away from the prevailing wind. This is necessary as the wind will help the skimmer to work by blowing any surface material towards it. Otherwise, the wind will blow the surface debris to one end while the skimmer will be at the other!

The skimmer needs to be as far as possible from the feeding area, as this will prevent it from collecting the food before the fish can find it.

Tip: If this proves a problem, it may be an advantage to install an on/off switch at the feeding point, so that you can turn off the skimmer while you feed the fish.

Always check that sealers and glues are compatible with the materials that you are using, as some contain solvents that could damage the pipe or liner. With sealers, check that they do not contain antimould additives, which are toxic to fish.

CHAPTER 8

LIGHTING

1. Types of light
2. Coloured lights
3. Transformers

There are a number of thoughts on underwater lighting. Some people believe that it upsets the fish and makes them nervous. However, there is little evidence to support this, and, providing the lighting is not excessive, the fish actually seem to enjoy it.

If you intend to install lighting but have yet to build your pond, remember to leave a conduit for the cables through the wall or under the paving. It will be much neater than leaving the cables lying in the water. You must also remember to build in a safe place for the transformer. Although some transformers are waterproof, it is better to have them in a dry place, as this makes maintenance so much easier.

A few carefully-placed lights can make a pond, so don't be afraid of trying the lights in different positions and with different coloured lenses until you find your perfect set-up.

TYPES OF LIGHT

Mains-powered lights are normally bulky and the light output is relativity poor for the size of the unit. In addition, fish can easily damage themselves on lights, so they should be placed away from the fish to avoid this happening. Low-voltage halogen lamps are safer and more efficient, using less energy. As a bonus, the bulbs usually last longer, too.

Check out the maximum number of lights you can run from one transformer. Some systems allow one to two lights only, while others can run up to six or more. The better-quality lights will have useful extras, such as focusing lenses and different bulb wattages. Some light sets allow the connection of external lights for the garden at the same time, but this means the pond and garden lights will always be on at the same time.

COLOURED LIGHTS

Different colours can be obtained by using one of two approaches – either exchanging the clear lens for a coloured one, or adding a coloured disc in front of the lens. Discs are only suitable for underwater use, as they can melt on the hot glass when out of the water.

TRANSFORMERS

Finally, when purchasing your lights, choose a transformer that will cope with extra lights in case you want to upgrade your system later on.

CHAPTER 9

SIMPLE WATER CHEMISTRY

1. pH
2. Temperature
3. Water hardness
4. Carbon dioxide and oxygen
5. Ammonia
6. Nitrite
7. Nitrate

The most important part of the pond, of course, is the water itself. A little knowledge of basic water chemistry, often referred to as water quality, is essential if you want to keep fish, and the general principles are described here.

In fishkeeping, there is really no such thing as a fishkeeper; the real job is keeping the pond water in a stable condition, within the tolerance of your fish. Fish can stand almost any change to their environment providing that change is slow.

It is very easy to check the water with a test kit (available from many garden centres and pet shops). They are quick and simple to use, and will provide you with an accurate guide to the environment within your pond. It is useful to keep a record of your results, so that, in the future, you will be able to compare test patterns and spot potential problems.

Get into the habit of using the same type of test kit each time, so that you get used to the procedure and analysing the result. Remember, test kits will go out of date once opened, and they will give false readings once their use-by date is exceeded.

pH

In simple terms, pH value is a way of indicating whether your pond water is acid, alkali, or neutral. pH is a measure of the proportion of hydrogen ions to hydroxyl ions. There are three categories into which the pH level of your pond water will fall:

- **Neutral:** When hydrogen and hydroxyl ions are present in equal numbers, water is neutral and is given a pH value of seven.
- **Acid:** When the hydrogen ions exceed the number of hydroxyl ions, the water becomes acidic and the value of the pH falls below seven.
- **Alkaline:** When the hydroxyl ions exceed the number of hydrogen ions, the water becomes alkaline and the pH rises above seven to a maximum of 14.

PH level	0-3	3-6.5	6.5-8.0	8-10.0	10-14.0
Category	Very acid	Acid	Ideal	Alkaline	Very alkaline

The ideal pH value for ponds is between 6.5 and 8. The pH measurement is logarithmic, which means that a one-point shift shows a tenfold change in their concentration. In simple terms, this means a small rise in pH actually reflects a large change in the balance of ions.

A number of things can affect the pH. Rainwater, for example, is low in minerals, so it tends to be acidic and therefore lowers the pH in your pond. The addition of calcium in the form of rockery stone or cement will have the opposite effect.

RAISING THE pH

In acidic ponds, the addition of calcium-based oyster shell or chalk will raise the pH. It is difficult to control how quickly the pH rises by this method, so add very small amounts at a time and keep retesting the water. You may find it simpler, though more expensive, to buy a pH-raising product which has been formulated and manufactured to do this job.

LOWERING THE pH

Lowering the pH is difficult, and, providing it is not too excessive (i.e. more than pH 9), the effort expended will not be reflected by an improvement in the health of your fish.

Very high pH is rare and can be solved by diluting the pond with water from your tap (faucet). Filtration through peat can also help to reduce the pH. However, it will also turn the water colour light brown. The larger the pond, the more difficult it is to control the pH value. Once again, specially manufactured products are available to lower pH.

TEMPERATURE

Water temperature in a pond changes very slowly, which is important for the fish. They take their temperature from the surrounding water and have little or no means to alter this. Therefore they are very susceptible to sudden thermal changes such as might occur when moving to a new pond. They are also at risk if they are in a comparatively small volume of water being affected by natural weather conditions, such as a small pond on a sunny day. Temperature changes in excess of 5 degrees Celsius (e.g. from 10-15 degrees Celsius/50-59 degrees Fahrenheit) can cause death. Fish are particularly susceptible to a sharp decrease in temperature, so always ensure your pond is deep enough to slow down the process.

Rapid changes that do not kill fish will still severely stress them, making them more susceptible to disease.

WATER HARDNESS

Water hardness is, in simple terms, the measure of concentration of certain minerals (particularly calcium) in the water. The measurement for hardness is generally in milligrammes per litre (mg/litre), as are measurements on all test kits. The chart below shows the 'scale' of hardness and relevant levels in both mg/litre

mg/litre CaCO3 (calcium)	dH	Levels considered
0-50	3	very soft
50-100	3-6	soft
100-200	6-12	slightly hard
200-300	12-18	fairly hard
300-450	18-25	hard
450+	25+	very hard

and dH (degrees hardness, which is a commonly used German measurement).

Water hardness affects freshwater fish by influencing the osmoregulation that fish use to maintain internal body chemistry. Hard water has a higher concentration of minerals, so the difference between a fish's internal systems and the surrounding water is small. On the other hand, fish in soft water, with a low concentration of salts, have to work harder to maintain a stable body chemistry. Fish also need calcium to build bones and to ensure the blood calcium-levels are constant.

Making water harder is easy. Simply add a calcium-based rock or oyster shell and check with a test kit until the desired level is achieved. Softening the water is more difficult. The safest method is to use a softening resin, such as those used in a conventional household water softener.

CARBON DIOXIDE AND OXYGEN

The main gases dissolved in water are carbon dioxide and oxygen. Carbon dioxide is the more soluble, and, therefore, its level is the highest. Submerged plants use it to produce oxygen and food, whereas animals consume oxygen and produce carbon dioxide as the waste product from this process.

Water can only hold a certain amount of oxygen at any temperature, but, as the temperature rises, the levels are reduced. The table below shows maximum levels in water at different temperatures, and the minimum levels required in ideal conditions by a goldfish.

Temp	5C/41F	10C/50F	15C/60F	20C/68F	25C/77F
Max level	12.8 mg/litre	11.3	10.2	9.2	8.2
Ideal conditions	9.1	8.8	8.3	7.8	7.4
% of saturation	71	78	84	85	90

BUILDING A GARDEN POND

Use sand to mark the outline of your pond. Stand back, assess it, and move the sand if you wish to amend the shape.

Remove the turf from the pond area and place it on polythene in case you need to use it later.

The different depths of the pond can be set using pegs.

BUILDING A GARDEN POND

Line the bottom of the hole with sand. Rake it over so you get a smooth, level surface that is free from sharp stones.

Split-log edging can be fitted to the perimeter of your pond to create a more formal look.

Put the pond liner in place, ensuring that it fits snugly into the hole.

BUILDING A GARDEN POND

Part-fill the pond with water, using a hose-pipe.

The liner can now be covered with rocks and/or the turf that was removed earlier.

Gather together your planting materials to begin decorating the pond area.

BUILDING A GARDEN POND

Most pond plants need to be rooted in soil, so plant them in baskets before submerging them.

Position your plants in the pond before completely filling it up with water.

The finished pond, with established vegetation.

FOUNTAIN FEATURES

The sound of running water creates a soothing atmosphere and can be achieved through a simple spray-jet (right), a formal fountain (middle), or a natural-looking waterfall (bottom).

SMALL BUT SWEET

You do not need a huge garden to have a pond.
With a little imagination, some great effects can be achieved.

A barrel can be
adapted as an
unusual patio
water feature.

A small, raised pond
can be built –
a safer option if you
have children or pets.

A 'bubble stone'
can be housed in
the smallest of
ponds, making an
attractive feature
where space is
limited.

STONE AGE

Rocks and stones can be used in a number of ways to decorate a pond, creating a natural-looking – and impressive – focal point.

BE INSPIRED!

A pond can be as simple or as complex as you wish –
you are limited only by your imagination.

As you can see, the level of saturation required rises with temperature. If you are keeping fish, it is important to keep oxygen levels high and carbon dioxide levels low.

Many people believe that pond plants can provide enough oxygen for the fish, but this is seldom true, as most ponds are stocked more densely than nature intended. Although plants produce oxygen during the day, they also consume oxygen at night, and levels can drop dangerously low, particularly on stormy nights when the natural level of oxygen in the air is low anyway.

There are several other factors which can also lead to low oxygen levels, such as poor filter design. The bacteria in filters require oxygen to live and to oxidise ammonia and nitrite. If the water flow is too slow, the bacteria will strip all the available oxygen from the water and it will return to the pond loaded with carbon dioxide.

Treating the pond with chemicals to kill parasites or algae will also lower the oxygen level.

LOW OXYGEN

The signs that indicate that oxygen levels in your pond are too low are similar to those caused by excessive ammonia. Therefore, if the following signs are evident, you need to check for both oxygen and ammonia levels.

- Fish mouthing at the surface. The highest concentration of oxygen is in the first 2 to 3 cm (0.8 to 1.2 inches) of water, and the fish will try to breathe in this layer.
- Fish congregating around water inlets or under fountains (circulated water normally contains more oxygen).
- Fish will be lethargic and they will hover near the surface.

QUICK CURES

- Add water from the tap after treating with a de-chlorinator. As it is cold, it will hold more oxygen and it will slow the fishes' metabolism, reducing their oxygen requirements.
- Increase water circulation with a water pump, or, better still, an air pump.
- Reduce feeding. Fish need oxygen to break down and to absorb food.
- Shade the pond from the sun if temperature is the cause.

- *Never* switch off pumps at night, especially during the summer.
- In warm weather, keep a spare air pump running, in case the main pump fails.
- Never overstock the pond.
- Reduce the load on the filter by cleaning the waste out regularly.
- Control the amount of oxygenating plants. They should never cover more than one-third of the pond surface.

AMMONIA

Ammonia is a by-product of the breakdown of protein (food) into energy, which the fish uses to grow and to maintain body functions. It is excreted as urine and through the gills in exchange for sodium as part of the ion regulation system. When dissolved in water, ammonia quickly changes to produce ammonium ions and hydroxyl ions. As the pH increases, more of this 'free' ammonia is formed. Even relatively low levels of ammonia can cause damage to sensitive parts of the fish, such as gills, fins and skin. It also impairs the blood's ability to carry oxygen.

The presence of ammonia also causes brain and central nervous problems, and encourages some diseases by weakening the fish, allowing an infection such as bacterial gill disease, dropsy, or fin rot to start.

In a biological filter, ammonia, in the presence of oxygen, is converted into nitrite by bacteria called nitrosomonas.

CAUSES OF HIGH AMMONIA

High ammonia can be caused by many factors, but some of the most common ones are listed below.

- The bio filter is immature and unable to cope with the fish population.
- Overfeeding the fish, which then produce more waste than the filter can process.
- Overstocking the pond.
- Some treatments for fish will kill off the filter bacteria, leading to the filter collapsing.
- Algae killers. Once the algae have died, they will start to rot and this will produce ammonia.
- Excessive waste on the pond floor will start to be broken down by bacteria and this will release ammonia and other toxic chemicals.

SIGNS OF AMMONIA POISONING

- Haemorrhaging of internal organs, bleeding from gills and around fins.
- Gills increased in size and pale in colour.
- Mucus coating on gills and fins reduces, and in some cases disappears.
- Fish become lethargic and hang around water inlets.
- Fins start to discolour and 'rot' towards the body.

SHORT-TERM CURES

If high ammonia occurs in your pond, it is essential you remove it quickly, as long-term exposure will be fatal to your fish.

- Change part of the water. Drain out 50 per cent of the pond and refill with de-chlorinated tap water, but do it slowly to avoid shocking the fish.
- If you are feeding your fish, stop immediately.
- Remove any debris from the base of the pond as you perform the water change.
- Always remove excess algae *before* treating.
- As ammonia is a gas in solution form, extra aeration will help to drive it off.
- Use zeolite, a natural rock that absorbs ammonia and other nitrogen compounds. Some types of zeolite can be recharged in a salt solution.
- Manufacturers have produced chemicals that will bond with ammonia, rendering it non-toxic. These work instantly.
- Add a starter biological culture.

NITRITE

Nitrite test kits will give you a measurement in mg per litre. Although less toxic than ammonia, nitrite is still harmful at relatively low levels (0.5mg/litre), and is lethal over 10 mg/litre. Nitrite in hard water is less toxic than in soft water.

Nitrite breaks down red blood cells by oxidising the iron, which then has no oxygen-carrying capacity. Nitrite is broken down by a nitrobacter and converted into nitrate in the filter.

Even very low levels of nitrite can lead to fish being more susceptible to disease and, ideally, the levels should be kept below 0.01mg/litre.

CAUSES OF NITRITE POISONING

- Poor filters are the major reason for high levels of nitrite. A poorly functioning filter will not break down the nitrite, and, in some cases, it may even turn nitrate (see below) back to nitrite.
- Overfeeding can result in a filter that cannot cope with the waste products.
- Treating the pond to kill algae can overload the filter.
- Some fish treatments will kill or damage the filter bacterial levels, stopping nitrite being converted to nitrate.

SIGNS OF NITRITE POISONING

The main symptoms are very similar to oxygen starvation – listlessness and hovering near the surface. The gills will turn a dark-brown colour from the iron-nitrite combination.

CURES

As with ammonia, the cure is based on the filter.

- If there is *no* ammonia present, add salt at 3 mg/litre. There is a downside to using salt, however, as it reduces the oxygen level in the water and will also affect the filter bacteria. Salt should only be used as a last resort if levels are very high.
- Do a number of water changes, 25 per cent at a time, to dilute the nitrite. Refill slowly to avoid shocking the fish.
- Clean out the filter and remove any sludge that has collected. Do not wash out the biological section with water from the household tap (faucet) as this will reduce the number of bacteria. Only use pondwater for cleaning.
- Add a live bacterial culture to boost the filter bacterial levels, and increase oxygenation (the new bacteria will need it to work).
- Turn off the UV light, as it will kill some of the bacteria passing through it to the filter.

NITRATE

Nitrate has very high limits of lethal toxicity, and for some species it is more than 1000 times less toxic than nitrite. Nitrate is more toxic to young fish and eggs than to adult fish. It has been suggested that a high level of nitrate can make fish more susceptible to disease, and can slow growth rates, but I am not convinced that this is true.

Nitrate test kits will give you a measurement in mg per litre. Nitrate is best kept below 150 mg/litre in a pond. The higher the level, the more food there will be for algae and you will get green water and blanket weed.

Nitrate is created by the bacteria in the filters, which convert ammonia to nitrite and then to nitrate. Whatever you do, nitrate is formed by this natural process, so there will always be some level of nitrate in the water; your job is to achieve and maintain a healthy level. Be aware that some areas have very high levels of nitrate in their mains water supply

SIGNS OF NITRATE POISONING
A high level of nitrate is very difficult to detect, so testing the water is the only really effective method.

REDUCING NITRATE
Nitrate levels can be reduced by making regular water changes, and use of an ion exchange resin similar to a water softener will help. However, the easiest, cheapest, and best method is the use of a vegetable filter. Pass water from the filter, where the nitrate is created, through a shallow pond or stream filled with fast-growing water plants. They will extract the nitrate they need to grow and naturally lower the levels.

WATER MYTHS
There are a number of myths about household mains water from the tap (faucet). Chlorine, copper and other heavy metals may all be present, but most of the 'dangers' are myths.

Take chlorine, for example. It is very dangerous to fish, but the chlorine in tap (faucet) water dissipates very quickly once in the open air. You can smell it in some water supplies. Its function is to kill bacteria in the water and levels are very low, otherwise it would affect humans who drank it. Once in the pond, the chlorine attacks the first organic substance it can find, which is usually small floating particles of dirt and plants. Nevertheless, many experts do recommend using a de-chlorinator before adding tap water to a pond. There are many on the market and they all work, as the chemicals are basic and reliable. If you feel safer using a de-chlorinator, then by all means do so.

Copper is often said to be very dangerous, even at low levels, but it is put in fish food (as copper sulphate) and it is the basic ingredient of some algaecides. It can affect some fish (such as sturgeon and trout) but the levels in tap (faucet) water are far too low to pose a danger.

Lead is very toxic, and, if you have any levels in your water, it will affect you as much as your fish, so get it checked out for your own safety.

There are many other metals that are often quoted as being dangerous, but most are necessary in small amounts for the metabolism of the fish. In fact, many fish-food producers now list the elements in their foods and most of them are toxic – but only at much higher levels.

The temperature of tap (faucet) water added to a pond is potentially a much more serious problem for the fish. The new water also has as an unstable pH and the oxygen levels are either supersaturated (i.e. it is holding more than would be possible normally as it has been under pressure in the pipework) or the level is very low due to the length of time spent in the pipework. This is why it is recommended that you leave the water to 'stand' for a few days.

MAINTAINING WATER QUALITY

While it is desirable to have 'perfect' water parameters, it is not always possible. Local water conditions may give you a higher or lower pH than is desirable. Rather than change the water conditions constantly, it is arguably better to have the most stable water conditions possible. This means the fish can acclimatise, and, generally, they will fare better for this. Constantly changing the conditions simply means the fish are endlessly having to readjust.

This is a good range for most pond fish:
- **pH:** 6.5 to 8
- **Oxygen level:** 7.5 mg/litre to saturation
- **Ammonia:** less than 0.1mg/litre
- **Nitrite:** less than 0.1mg/litre
- **Nitrate:** less than 150mg/litre
- **Hardness:** 100 to 400 mg/litre.

CHAPTER 10

YOUR FISH

FEEDING AND DAILY CARE

Fish will get used to set feeding times and, if you feed at the same hour each day, after a while they will be waiting for you! In a natural pond, fish feed most of the day, and, because of this, nature designed them with a digestive system that was built for 'little and often' feeding. It is best, therefore, to feed small quantities, two to three times a day. Most fish will eat as much as you can feed them, but excess food is wasted and will upset the water quality.

The food you buy will directly affect your fish's health and growth rate. Flake food is good for small fish up to four cm (1.5 inches), but larger fish need a more substantial food, such as floating sticks or pellets. Lower-priced foods tend to have low protein levels and this will slow the growth of the fish, so they are unsuitable for faster-growing species such as orfe or koi.

A good-quality food for koi is a must, as it will contain extra minerals and vitamins, as well as colour enhancers. In my experience, these rarely enhance the colours, but they do slow the natural fading that occurs as fish grow older.

Although most foods are sold as a complete feed, you should mix two or three different ones to ensure that a more balanced diet is achieved. Buy small packs that you can use before they go out of date. Bigger bags may seem better value, but the food will start to lose vitamins as soon as it is opened.

If you must buy in bulk, either share it with another fishkeeper or split it into smaller bags and store sealed until needed.

BUYING YOUR FIRST FISH

The first thing you need to determine is the number of fish your pond will support. The ratio of fish to water is normally worked out using the following simple rule: 3 cm (1.25 inches) of fish per 50 litres (11 UK gallons or 13 US fluid gallons) of water with filtration, half this without.

For example, a 2,000-litre (440-UK-gallon or 525-US-fluid-gallon) pond will support 120 cm (50 inches) of fish (the equation is 2000/50 x 3 in metric, 440/11 x 1.25 in UK imperial, or 525/13 x 1.25 in US imperial). If you stick to this rule, you should have a trouble-free experience, but remember to allow room for growth, so only stock to half this level.

> *Tip: If you are going to keep large-growing species (such as sturgeon), you will need to double the volume, so 100 litres (22 UK gallons or 26.5 US fluid gallons) per 3 cm (1.25 inches) is the benchmark.*

Before leaving to buy fish, check your pond water to make sure it is within normal quality parameters, or take a sample with you for your retailer to check. Take a box or container to put the bag of fish into, as this will stop it rolling around in the car, and a blanket to cover the fish as they travel better in the dark.

Your first fish should be introduced at least 4 weeks after you have planted the pond. This allows the plants to settle down and grow before the fish start eating them.

Start with a few hardy fish such as goldfish or shubunkins. When these have settled for a few weeks without problems, you can purchase more to go into a quarantine tank. Do not stock the pond to its maximum level straight away. A few at a time is the best and safest way.

CHOOSING YOUR FISH

Choosing your fish from the retailer can pose problems. Not all sell good-quality or well-cared-for fish, so, when you find a good retailer, stick with him. Buying fish from many different retailers increases the chance of infecting your pond with disease.

Look out for the following signs:

- Are the fish huddled in a corner motionless? This is not a good sign, as it can mean they are sick or new in. The exception is tench, as this is normal behaviour for the species.
- Are there any dead fish? If the retailer cannot be bothered to remove dead fish, there is little chance he can be bothered to treat fish well. Walk away.
- Are the fish at the surface looking for food? This normally shows they are being fed, as they associate people with food.
- Do the fish have any marks or fungus on them? Because of the medium fish live in (i.e. water), disease spreads very quickly. Any fish sharing a system with sick fish will catch the same disease, although they may not show it. Do not buy from tanks if sick fish are present.
- Ask to see the fish feed. If they don't feed, they could be ill or new imports so it is best to leave them alone.
- Once the fish have been caught and packed in a *clean*, clear plastic bag, check them again. If they are skinny, or have any marks, don't accept them.
- Take the fish straight home. The shorter the time the fish are in the bag, the better.

> *Tip: Always try to buy locally bred fish, as they will be used to your water conditions and climate. They should also be less prone to disease as they have had less stress getting to the shop.*

INTRODUCING THE FISH

The first fish you buy can go straight into the pond, but subsequent fish should be quarantined. The process of acclimatising fish to either your pond or a quarantine tank is the same. The less the shock, the better for the fish.

Take the fish to your pond and float the bag for 15-20 minutes to allow the temperature to equalise. In very sunny weather, do not leave the bag in direct sunlight. Always offer shade – an umbrella on the side of the pond will do. Open the bag and pour in from the pond about half as much water as is already in the bag. Leave for another 15 to 20 minutes. This allows the fish to get used to your water chemistry.

If possible, gently net the fish, take them out and place them in the pond. Lift out the bag of water and dispose of it away from the pond. This will prevent any medications the shop uses from entering your water. Let the new fish settle for a few days before trying to feed them. If you take sick fish home, they will either die or infect your other fish, or both. Both scenarios are upsetting and unnecessary if you follow these simple guidelines.

QUARANTINE

Quarantine your fish before you put them in the pond. There is no better way to protect your fish stock than to keep your new fish in quarantine for at least eight weeks.

The possible consequences of putting new fish straight into your pond make a quarantine tank look like a cheap option, and, once your fish collection builds up in size, it will be even better value.

BASIC QUARANTINE TANK

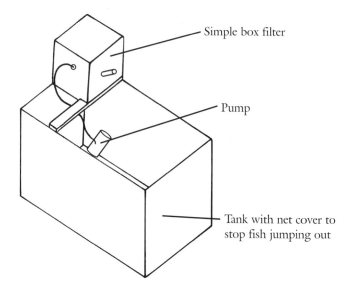

Simple box filter

Pump

Tank with net cover to stop fish jumping out

A basic quarantine tank need only be a loft water tank (for smaller fish) and a simple box filter and pump with an air pump as back-up. Remember to place the tank out of direct sunlight and in a sheltered spot to stop the wind chilling the water. Indoors is better still, either in a garden shed or garage. A small heater is a good investment as you can keep the fish at a constant temperature, which will help to reduce stress.

Do regular water changes and keep an eye on the water quality readings. The better the water, the better the fish will be when the quarantine period is over.

If, for one reason or another, you cannot quarantine fish, then you must be as certain as possible that they come from a reputable source. Don't be afraid to ask your retailer about his own quarantine 'rules' and, if you are not satisfied, buy elsewhere.

SPECIES OF FISH

If you plan to keep more than one species, you need to be certain they are compatible. There would be no point in keeping pike with goldfish, for obvious reasons, but, likewise, keeping minnows with koi is a mistake. The koi will eat them if they can catch them. So decide what sort of fish you would like and do not be swayed into an impulse purchase because something looked 'cute'. This can lead to disastrous results.

It is not advisable to mix young fish with larger, mature fish as they may be hounded by the larger fish and hide to the point of starving to death because they are too afraid to feed. If your budget will run only to small fish, you can always grow them on in another, smaller pond, or even in the quarantine tank, until they are large enough to stay out of trouble.

The most important thing to remember is not to make price the most significant factor when buying a fish. The most important question is 'Do you like it?' After all, you will be the one who is looking at the fish.

GOLDFISH (CARASSIUS AURATUS)

Without doubt, the number one fish for many pondkeepers. It is very hardy, can tolerate almost any conditions and yet still looks colourful and healthy. It is originally from China, where records show it being bred about 400AD. It now comes in many shapes and sizes, from the common goldfish we all know, to the more exotic-looking Chinese and Japanese orandas.

Goldfish can grow to 40 cm (16 inches) or more, but, normally, 30 cm (12 inches) is classed as a large specimen. They are easy to look after, and, providing the initial stock is disease-free, they will stay in perfect health with little help.

Goldfish breed very quickly. In cooler climates, the fry are uncoloured until they reach 6 to 10 cm (3 to 4 inches) in length, when they start to change to bright red/orange. Some fish will stay black all their lives and are best removed, as eventually they will take over the pond and outgrow and outfeed the coloured ones.

If your fish breed every year, reduce the numbers to keep stocking levels under control. This not only helps the other fish to grow, but also allows the filter, if you have one, and plants, to keep up with the waste that the fish produce.

COMET

Similar to a normal goldfish, but with longer, flowing fins. It is not quite as hardy, but, in deeper ponds, it will survive in all but the coldest winters.

The comet comes in other colours, such as the red-and-white sarasa comet. The best of these come from Japan. A black-and-red colour is sometimes seen on smaller fish, but the black changes to red as the fish grows into a normal comet.

SHUBUNKIN

In more recent times, the goldfish has become multi-coloured, with a mixture of blues, reds, orange, black, and white, called the shubunkin. With its large comet tail and flowing fins, it is a truly pretty fish and a good stand-in for koi in smaller ponds. It will cross-breed with the normal goldfish, but most of the young will be black.

ORANDAS

There are many varieties in the oranda group, but they are not suitable for ponds in cold winters. They need to be moved indoors for the winter and then moved back to the pond for the summer. They do not mix well with other types of goldfish, so should be kept with their own kind.

KOI

Originally from Japan, they are now bred in many countries, but the Japanese still produce the best specimens. Koi are coloured carp, so they exhibit the same general behaviour patterns and characteristics. They can grow very large given space and food, and fish in excess of one metre (3 feet) long are not uncommon. However, the average size of a mature koi is 60 cm (2 feet). Japanese fish still seem to grow larger than those from other countries, probably because they come from better brood stock and because the selection process for the young is more efficient.

Koi can live for up to 70 years, but 20 years is nearer the average. Once they are settled in the pond, nothing seems to worry them, and, in time, they will become hand-tame in exchange for food.

However, koi are a major cause of problems for the new pondkeeper. They have become weaker than the original carp because of selection and cross-breeding for colours and patterns. Therefore, they are more susceptible to disease. Due to the modern way of moving fish about, and the 'just in time' stocking policy most shops have adopted, the fish are not allowed to rest for any length of time to recover from the stress and strain of the journey and to start feeding. So fish are sold unrested and stressed – not ideal. This leads to problems for the fishkeeper. Buy with caution and always quarantine new fish.

There is a large variety of different coloured koi and all have names to describe the colours and patterns. For a better understanding of the colours and patterns, you should buy a specialist book on koi.

There are many myths about the difficulties of keeping koi and their special requirements, but, in fact, they are very easy to look after and very hardy. Some of the myths include:

- **Koi must have filtered water.** Although clear water is a good thing for us, koi prefer a muddy, cloudy pond to root around in. This is why koi farms grow their fish in mud ponds, not clear-filtered ones.

- **Koi must have deep water to get the correct body shape.** Unfortunately, koi, like us, must rely on two more important influences that will dictate their body shape: what the parents look like (genetics) and what they eat. If you look at your fish as they grow, you will notice that they don't all grow at the same rate or to the same shape. If water depth was a major factor in body shape, all fish would grow to much the same shape in the same depth. They don't!

- **You must only feed specialist foods.** Koi are omnivores and will eat almost anything. In a natural pond, their main diet would consist of small insects, snails and some vegetation. It is a good idea to mix different foods, as most are not a complete feed as the manufacturers would have you believe. Koi will also eat oranges, peaches, breakfast cereals (especially the ones with honey on them!), brown bread, cooked green peas, sweetcorn, liver, worms, fishing maggots and just about any other food you can think of. If in doubt, try a small amount first. If they don't eat it, remove it before it pollutes the water. Never feed them on just one type of food. Vary it. Just like us, they get bored with the same diet.

COMMON CARP (CYPRINUS CARPIO)

They are the ancestors of koi, but, unlike koi, they are not colourful and not the ideal fish for a planted pond. They are very active diggers and will disturb, if not destroy, all planted baskets. They are unsuitable for small ponds due to their size.

Carp are very competitive feeders and will muscle their way in to get as much food as possible, often at the expense of more timid fish. They quickly grow very large, but have a calming effect on the other fish and can become very friendly. They are best kept in large unplanted or natural ponds, where they will flourish.

GHOST CARP

One of the first koi varieties to become really popular with the general pondkeeper, it was originally a cross between the common carp and an ogon (a metallic-yellow koi) which produced a dark bronze-coloured fish with a lighter golden head and skeletal pattern down its back.

Recently, more koi producers are selling poor-grade koi as ghost carp (notably, not the Japanese), in order to avoid running a proper selection process, where this type of fish would be eliminated. Ghost carp can grow to a large size and tend to dig up plants, so they are best suited to an unplanted pond or a lake.

GRASS CARP (CTENOPHARYNGODON IDELLA)

A true herbivore, they are a problem in planted ponds as they will eat nearly all vegetation. The most common form seen for sale is the albino, which has pale orange skin and red eyes. The normal variety is olive green in colour. They are often sold as a cure for blanket weed, but they seem to have little effect on the growth.

The grass carp can grow very large and is quite frenetic, rushing around the pond at the slightest movement or sound. It disturbs the other fish and sometimes jumps right out of the pond.

It is normally used to clear lakes of oxygenators, as in summer it can eat more than its own body weight of vegetation each day. It requires a licence in most countries and must never be released in native waters.

TENCH (TINCA TINCA)

The tench is one of the least known and seen pond fish, although it is very useful to have in the pond as it spends most of its time digging through the debris on the bottom looking for food. This stops the debris turning toxic by letting fresh water and oxygen reach all the media. It is available in various colours. The most common is green, the natural colour, but, the gold variety is one of the best-looking fish you can have in a small pond.

Tench breed when they are about 20 cm (8 inches) in size and require a well-planted pond. The young have a poor survival rate, so they are unlikely to overrun the pond. They will become tame after a time, especially if offered worms and other live foods.

Life expectancy can be up to 20 years. They can attain a length of 60 cm (2 feet) in the correct conditions, and do best when sharing with few other species, as they tend to be shy feeders. They will eat any dry food and surface feed, but prefer sinking food and live food such as worms or maggots. Other favourites are sweetcorn and wholemeal bread.

ORFE (LEUCISCUS IDUS)

The orfe, more often called the golden orfe, is a selected form of the original colour, which was a dark grey/black with a silver/white underside. Orfe are also available in blue and pink, although the colour is not reliable and they often revert to orange.

Fast-moving, active fish, they like to be in a shoal, feeding on the surface by snatching food as they swim past. They will take most floating foods and like to jump for flying insects.

They also like a high oxygen level, which makes them unsuitable for small ponds without a pump or air pump. Orfe can grow to 90 cm (3 feet) or more. They look thin from above, but hide a deep body below.

Orfe like to swim upstream if they can, so waterfalls are a temptation they cannot resist if the flow is sufficient.

They will breed when 30 cm (12 inches) or larger in a fast-flowing area such as a waterfall. Survival rate is good, due to the large size of the fry when born.

They are a species sold for all ponds, but they really do not achieve their potential unless in a large pond and in reasonably large numbers. They are best not mixed with koi, as they are nervous fish and can stop the koi becoming tame. Also, they cannot be treated with some koi remedies.

They are a good addition to a predominantly goldfish pond, as they add movement – even in winter when other fish are hibernating.

BITTERLING (RHODEUS ARAMUS)
They are rarely seen for sale, but bitterling are good fish for small patio ponds. They do not grow too large (reaching about 10 cm or 4 inches) and they are highly active fish, providing movement and interest.

The male is considerably more colourful than the female, often showing metallic red, blue/purple and green, especially during the breeding season. They breed in the pond by laying eggs into swan mussels for protection until the fry are about four weeks old, when they are released from the mussel. As the breeding method is unusual, they will not overpopulate the pond.

Bitterling prefer a well-planted pond with some clear swimming areas. The bitterling's preferred diet is small insects, but they will take flake food and mini-pellets. They will mix with any fish.

GOLDEN RUDD (SCARDINEUS ERYTHROPTHALMUS)
A truly active but nervous fish that can unsettle calmer species such as koi. Most often seen as the golden form, but, like the orfe, the natural fish is darker and less conspicuous. They are not

recommended for small ponds as they are very quick feeders, they breed very successfully, and they generally take over to the point of starving out the other fish. They will eat any food, floating or sinking.

GOLDEN MINNOW (PHOXINUS PHOXINUS)
An excellent fish for the smaller pond, due to its active nature and because, unlike other active fish, it does not unsettle other species as it is so small.

The golden minnow mixes well with smaller fish and does not damage plants, as it is a mid-water feeder looking for insects. It thrives in shoals of 5 or more and breeds well in ponds, provided that there are not many larger fish to eat the fry.

The golden minnow grows only to 10 cm (4 inches), so is ideal for patio ponds and small raised ponds – a good substitute for golden orfe in these environments.

It prefers live or frozen food, but will accept dry food such as flake or micro-pellets. Life expectancy is around five years, which is short for coldwater fish. The minnow needs to be protected from very cold weather. Use a small pond heater in extreme weather, or bring your fish into an aquarium indoors or tank in a frost-free greenhouse until spring.

ACIPENSER, STURGEON AND STERLETS
This family of fish are, without doubt, oversold – as a cure for blanket weed and cleaning the bottom of ponds, neither of which they achieve. In fact, they are carnivores and are quite difficult to keep in good condition. However, once settled and feeding, they are quite fascinating and are one of my top fish, especially the sterlet. Never buy small specimens as they are very difficult to get to feed. If they have been starved and are thin, they seldom recover, so get the best, healthy fish from the start.

Their natural habitat is large rivers and the sea, although they are quite happy to lead a freshwater-only life. They must have flowing water in ponds, as this means they can rest on the bottom without having to swim around to get oxygen. They also need plenty of swimming space. Cool water temperatures, ideally below 20 degrees Celsius (68 degrees Fahrenheit), and shade from the sun in summer are other requirements.

As they are not related to other pond fish, they don't suffer the same diseases and are almost immune to parasites even when other fish are covered in them. Your pond needs to be free of blanket weed, as these fish get tangled very easily and cannot back out. Neither do they tolerate some chemicals that are used for treating koi and other fish.

STERLET (ACIPENSER RUTHENUS)

This is a newcomer to the pond market, and great care should be taken when buying it. The siberian sturgeon *(Acipenser baerii)* is often sold as a 'sterlet' but it grows to 2 metres (over six feet) or more and is not a practical fish for the average garden pond. You can distinguish the sterlet by the white edges on its fins and nose, and dark grey skin with white along the lateral line. The sturgeon has a brown-tinted skin and no white edges to its fins, but quite often a white nose.

Sterlet are most active from dusk till dawn and during colder weather. They do not like high temperatures because this lowers the oxygen content of the water and they must have flowing water and plenty of swimming space. As bottom feeders, they must be fed sinking food, ideally high in oil and protein.

Sterlet are suitable for large ponds only (more than 10,000 litres or 2,200 UK gallons or 2,642 US fluid gallons) as they grow to 125 cm (4 feet) and 16 kgs (35 lbs) in weight. They will mix with any fish, but have been known to eat small tench.

The sterlet is an excellent pond fish as it is hardy, grows slowly and does not have the bony plates of other related species, so it is less likely to get stuck in blanket weed. Look out for the albino, which has yellow/orange skin and red eyes. They are very pretty and quite rare.

SIBERIAN STURGEON (ACIPENSER BAERII)

The siberian sturgeon is suited only to large ponds because of its size. It is a bottom feeder with a large appetite and will grow up to 50 cm (20 inches) a year in good conditions.

It prefers moving water, high levels of oxygen and a low water temperature to do well. A good-quality, sinking food is essential. Silver specimens are available sometimes and are very attractive.

GOLD SPOT/DIAMOND STURGEON (ACIPENSER GUELDENSTAEDTI)

The gold spot sturgeon is one of the largest-growing freshwater fish, which can reach 4.6 metres (15 feet) in length. It is not the best fish for garden ponds as it stresses easily and is very intolerant of high water temperatures and low oxygen. It mixes well with other fish, but gets stuck easily in blanket weed and often dies because of this. Very sharp bony scutes on the body can inflict damage on the unwary fishkeeper.

Some of these species may be covered by the Import of Live Fish Act in parts of the UK, and you may need a special licence to keep them (although private collections do not need a licence). Ask your retailer and if in doubt, contact the Environment Agency.

Other fish that require a licence, such as catfish, pike, perch and pumpkinseed, should never be placed in a garden pond. They are sometimes seen for sale in aquatic shops, but they all show predatory habits.

CHAPTER 11

PROTECTING YOUR FISH

Once you have built your fish collection, you need to protect it from outside predators such as cats or heron, otherwise it will simply dwindle away.

The simplest form of protection is a net across the pond. It is not the most attractive feature, but it is relatively foolproof and easy to install. The holes in the net must be 25 mm (about 1 inch) or smaller, otherwise it will be possible for predators to pull the fish through the holes and out of the pond. The net must be installed so that it is in tension (i.e. it is being stretched). If the net sags into the water, a heron will simply stand on it until it sinks down into the pond and then it will be able to stab the fish through the net. It may not be able to get the fish out, but it could still damage or kill them.

The best way to achieve a tight-fitting net is by drilling into the edge of the paving or rockwork around the pond and inserting a stainless steel hook. Position two opposite each other and then run a length of strong wire between them. Fix at both ends, making the wire as tight as possible. This will act as a support for the net, but don't leave loose ends hanging in the water as fish could damage themselves on them. The net then needs to be laid over the support wires and fixed at the hooks.

PROTECTION

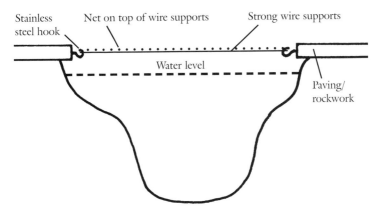

When plants grow up through the net, it will need to be moved so that it is in front of the plant but still leaves no gaps for access to the pond. Netting the pond is intrusive and a nuisance if you want to do any work on the pond, but it works very well, and gives the added bonus of stopping leaves falling in during winter.

Another way to protect your fish is to erect a small fence around the pond, which will put off most predators. It is also possible to use three or four strands of wire or fishing line to discourage heron, but this will not stop cats.

FENCING AGAINST PREDATORS

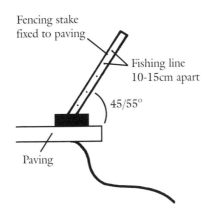

The fence needs to be a minimum height of 60 cm (2 feet) to stop tall herons leaning over the top and fishing. The height can be reduced if the fence is made to lean over the pond at a 45- to 55-degree angle. This also stops dogs and cats drinking from the pond, which is a good idea if you ever have to treat the fish.

This type of protection allows the plants to grow up without any interference from the fence and allows easier access to the pond for general work.

The fence cannot stop smaller flying predators, such as kingfishers or seagulls.

CHILDREN AND PONDS

The only way to be certain of stopping small children falling in is to fence off the entire pond area with a child-proof fence and a lockable gate. In any case, children should never be left near ponds without adult supervision.

All electrical supplies should be on a trip switch, or, if low-voltage products are available, use these instead.

Before buying a trip switch, ensure it is suitable for ponds. Many do not restart after a power cut, which means that the pond pump will not come back on. This could lead to fish dying through lack of oxygen.

CHAPTER 12

DISEASE IN FISH

The most common reason for fish becoming ill is the introduction of new fish that are either carrying or suffering from disease at the time of introduction. It is the major cause of fish mortality in the water garden, and the only way to protect your fish stock is to quarantine new arrivals before you put them in the pond.

RECOGNISING FISH PROBLEMS

The most important aspect of fishkeeping is the prevention and treatment of disease. It is relatively easy to get a post mortem examination on a dead fish, but your skill is to diagnose a problem from visible symptoms in the living creature.

There is no such thing as a completely disease-free fish. All will carry some disease or parasite, but remain quite tolerant unless they are put under stress or exposed to poor conditions or inadequate diet. Then you get problems, which we shall define as acute or chronic.

Acute problems occur when all fish show the same symptoms and the disease generally covers all species of fish in the pond, perhaps being measured as a change in behaviour rather than visible individual symptoms. Nearly always acute problems point towards environmental or water-quality problems, such as poor filtration, low oxygen levels or an external toxin.

Chronic conditions can take a long time to reveal themselves, and often spread slowly through one species at a time. Infectious diseases or parasites are usually to blame.

The first sign of a problem will be unusual behaviour or obvious visual symptoms, such as white spots. Many diseases are visible to the naked eye or with the use of a small, low-powered magnifying glass. Fish behaving strangely should be placed in a tank, preferably glass so that it is possible to see the fish from all angles. This will help to diagnose the problem without stressing the fish more than is necessary.

The most frequent cause of problems is poor water quality, but causes can also include underfeeding, overfeeding, poor diet or even fish attacking each. Other common reasons are poor aeration in warm weather and inconsistent filtration, often caused by not running the filter 24 hours a day.

Unfortunately, the first time most fishkeepers realise their fish are ill is when they start to die. Never treat on the off-chance that you may have the right product for the cure. Always find the cause of the problem before you treat, as this will not only save you time and money but will probably save lives.

Do not wait until more fish die. It is often better to take a fish that is unwell to specialists to check before the fish dies, as it will start to rot and degrade immediately. Once this has occurred, it becomes more and more difficult to find the cause.

DISEASE DIAGNOSIS

Observation is the best defence against problems spreading through the pond. There are many behavioural patterns in fish that have a problem, the most common being:

- A fish hanging lifeless in the water
- A fish remaining separated from the others in the pond for extended periods
- A fish constantly scratching (often called 'flashing') itself on objects in the pond
- A fish resting under a waterfall or near fountains

- A fish lying on the bottom with its fins clamped to its sides
- Slow deliberate breathing
- Very fast breathing
- Mouthing the surface water
- A fish lying on its side
- A fish taking food and then rejecting it uneaten.

VISIBLE PROBLEMS

The most obvious and easiest disease to spot on fish is infestation by skin parasites. The majority of them are visible to the naked eye. The following lists the most common parasites and skin complaints found on freshwater fish.

- **White spot:** Small, white spots the size of a grain of salt all over the fins and body of the fish.
- **Velvet disease:** A thin film of gold specks on the skin and fins. Mucus peeling away in long, ribbon-like strips.
- **Anchor worm:** Thin parasites up to 2 cm (0.8 inches) long, embedded in the skin of the fish. Normally seen between scales or at the base of fins. Anchor worm is quite distinctive as it often has two egg sacs at the rear end.
- **Cotton wool (cotton) disease:** A fungus that looks like cotton wool (cotton) stuck across the body of the fish. Fungus is normally a secondary infection to ulcers or wounds previously inflicted.
- **Leeches:** These are not as common as people think, but they will prey on sick or weak fish. Normally translucent, light to dark brown in colour, and often with stripes, they grow to 5 cm (2 inches) and generally attach themselves to areas with high blood flows, such as fins or the mouth area.
- **Fish lice:** Small, round, jelly-like discs up to 1 cm (0.5 inches) in diameter. They have large, visible eyes. Their favourite feeding places are around the base of the fins and under the body, where they are difficult to spot.
- **Gill maggots:** Very difficult to see, but the damage they cause to the gills can be seen as the fish breathes through the gill flap.
- **Swollen abdomen and dropsy:** Also called pinecone disease. The scales stick out from the body and take the shape of a pinecone.

- **Fin rot:** The fins split, turn pale or white and slowly rot towards the base of the fin where rot then starts to attack the body.
- **Fish pox:** Also called carp pox on koi. Large, waxy, creamy-white lumps normally found on the skin and fins. They sometimes take on the colour of the underlying tissue.
- **Ulcer disease:** A hole will normally appear through the scales. The flesh looks like it has been scooped out with a spoon.
- **Wasting disease or TB:** The fish becomes thinner and thinner, even though it eats, and the eyes sink into the head.

Having decided what the problems are and what the symptoms suggest, the following information will be useful to understand and cure each problem.

ANCHOR WORM

Anchor worm are easy to spot as they are very thin. They attach themselves under the scales with an anchor-shaped hook and you can usually see two egg sacs at the posterior end.

Quite often, the wound creates an opening to secondary infection and therefore the condition must be treated as soon as possible. When large numbers are present they can cause loss of weight and even death.

The parasite most often arrives with new fish, especially fancy goldfish and koi. It is quite difficult to control in a pond without the use of organophosphate insecticides, many of which are now banned.

The adults need to be removed as soon as possible in order to stop the egg sacs being released and eggs hatching. It is only the females that attack the fish. Males have a short lifespan and, once they have mated, they die. Use an organophosphate insecticide to kill the free-living juveniles.

The only way to deal with the adults is to manually remove each parasite with tweezers. Hold the worm firmly near the anchor, which is embedded in the fish, push it into the fish's body and then pull it up and out. The anchor should come out without too much problem. Once the parasite has been removed, treat the surrounding area with a good antiseptic.

The life cycle of the anchor worm means that manual removal

will need to be repeated after 10 to 15 days.

Before treating the pond with an organophosphate, be aware that many fish do not tolerate this chemical and veterinary advice should be taken.

COTTON WOOL (COTTON) DISEASE

Probably the easiest disease to see and diagnose, it can occur anywhere on the body. The fungus is normally a secondary infection to physical damage or ulcers. Other major triggers for fungus are poor water quality, overstocking, and unsuitable water conditions such as high pH or high ammonia levels.

Treatment is simple in the early stages, as the fungus is normally confined to the exterior of the fish. Treatments are malachite green, acriflavine and salt. If the fungus has spread to internal organs, it is probably too late. You can try an antibiotic, but it is rarely successful due to the internal damage inflicted by the fungus.

DROPSY OR PINECONE DISEASE

There are many causes of dropsy, from bacterial infection to poor nutrition. Unfortunately, it is often very difficult to find out the cause of the problem before it is too late. The main symptoms for dropsy are a swollen body, protruding scales, reddening at the vent area or base of fins, and, often, it is accompanied by ulcers on the body.

The fish showing signs of dropsy will go off their food and sometimes the skin will darken. The eyes may stick out due to fluid accumulating behind them, and this is often called 'pop eye'.

Poor water quality, low-quality food, and poor husbandry skills are usually to blame for the problem.

Treatment is very difficult, but proprietary treatments are available. If they do not work, you may need an antibiotic. Affected fish should be quarantined and treated away from other fish to avoid the infection spreading.

FIN ROT

The obvious symptoms are split fins with a white translucent edge to them. It is usually caused by bacteria, often after the fish has been damaged by rough handling, overcrowding, poor water quality or overfeeding, which can lead to the filter failing to cope.

Many goldfish of the large, long-finned varieties can suffer from this, especially in very cold winters, so take particular care if you keep fancy goldfish. Treatment is quite simple if the problem is caught early enough. A general antibacterial treatment will do the trick in most cases. More severe outbreaks will require antibiotics in order to control the problem. As with many diseases, water quality is likely to be a key factor, and should be checked.

FISH LICE

This large, jelly-like disc is in fact a crustacean, and is easy to detect. It attaches itself to the skin by means of two suckers and feeds by piercing the skin of the fish and drinking its blood. Lice can cause great irritation to fish, and the fish will often scratch to try to dislodge them. This can be a cause of other problems, as fish often damage themselves in the process.

Although not a severe problem to large fish, lice in relatively large numbers can kill small fish. They can also pass on any blood-borne diseases or bacteria as they suck the blood.

Treatment is similar to anchor worm. The fish need to be taken from the water and the lice removed with tweezers. The pond may also need to be treated with an organophosphate to control the free-swimming juveniles, so seek veterinary advice. Fish lice are not normally seen during the winter months, but in summer they can multiply very quickly if left unchecked.

GILL MAGGOTS

Fortunately, gill maggots are rarely seen, but they are a major problem if they do occur in your pond as they are difficult to treat and can spread extremely quickly among fish.

The female is seen on the fish, always on the gills, attached by hooks and often with two egg sacs hanging from the rear. The male parasite only lives until it mates. Gill maggots are about one millimetre long, plus the egg sacs.

The only effective treatment is to use an organophosphate insecticide or potassium permanganate.

The parasite is also controlled by temperature. It stops reproducing below 14 degrees Celsius (57 degrees Fahrenheit), but, the warmer the water becomes, the quicker it spreads. The life cycle can be broken by removing the fish from the pond for two to three weeks in warm weather, so that any eggs will hatch and the free-swimming larvae will die if they cannot find a fish host.

Treat the pond at least twice to make sure any adults are killed off, and treat fish outside the pond in a separate tank.

GILL PROBLEMS

Most gill problems are caused by bacterial infections, fungus and parasites. All of these can be avoided with simple, water-quality management.

Fish have their own defence mechanisms to combat most things, but when conditions deteriorate they become susceptible and, as the gills are the most sensitive part of the fish, they are always first to suffer.

Most obvious symptoms include excessive gill movements, lethargic fish on the base of the pond or at the surface, swollen or discoloured gill filaments and excess mucus production. The fish will also be off their food.

As water quality is often the cause, check this first and, if necessary, change the water. If possible, take the fish to a dealer so that he can diagnose the problem, and suggest a treatment. Do not attempt to treat the fish until you are sure of the cause of the problem.

GILL BACTERIA

The use of a good, broad-spectrum antibacterial treatment, such as an antibiotic, is required to control bacterial infections. Remember, when fish have gill problems, they will require extra aeration, as it is difficult for them to absorb oxygen with damaged gills.

GILL FLUKES

Two types affect pond fish. The most common, and problematical, is the dactylogyridae family. The second, the gyrodactylidae family, is rarely seen on the gills and is more often on the body and fins of the fish. Under a microscope, flukes are easy to distinguish. They have a sucker and a four-pointed anterior end. The caudal end holds one or two pairs of attaching hooks.

Young fish are the most susceptible to infestations of flukes, and it is a very virulent parasite. The gills of the fish are irritated to a point where they swell and become inflamed. This can lead to a thickening of the gill filaments, a defensive reaction which forces the parasite to the outer part of the gills.

Dactylogyrus have a relatively short lifespan, but multiply quickly. Eggs hatch in two to three days in the summer, and the larvae attach themselves to the fish straightaway and move around the host's body in a similar fashion to a caterpillar. Their main diet is the blood of the host and, if numbers are great enough, this can lead to nutritional problems for the fish and eventually death.

Treatment is easy if the condition is caught in time. Use salt (sodium chloride), potassium permanganate or formalin. In difficult cases, organophosphates can be used, but only with great care.

GILL ROT

Gill rot is the name given to a fungal infection that turns the gills to a yellow-brown colour. Soon after the infection, the gills start to disintegrate. The most common times for infection are after long, warm periods, when water quality has suffered and oxygen levels have fallen. Small fish are very susceptible to gill rot and do not recover easily.

The fish show signs by gasping for air at the surface and from the discoloration of the gill filaments. The fungus spore drives a tube into the gill and sends out hyphae (root-like appendages) to absorb the tissue. As the blood flow is reduced, the gills 'rot' and large sections fall away. The spread is very rapid in conditions where the population is high, the temperature is warm, and algae growth and organic loads (suspended waste) are excessive. Good water flow, low fish density and good water conditions will save all but the worst-affected fish.

Treatments for gill rot, such as copper sulphate, are very difficult to use safely, so advice should be sought. Malachite green, although not as effective, can be used in the early stages and will normally suffice.

GILL MUCUS

Although not a disease or parasite, it is always a bad sign if the fish start to produce excessive mucus from the gills, as this indicates either chemical toxins in the water, such as ammonia or nitrite, or an external chemical (e.g. weedkiller) or parasites.

The mucus appears from behind the operculum (gill cover) in thin, translucent-white strips that float in the water, still attached to the fish.

SKIN PROBLEMS

The skin of the fish is open to attack from many parasites and the fish defends itself by producing mucus, similar to that from the gills. The mucus is lost in normal swimming, and, as it falls away, the parasites are shed. When defending themselves, the mucus thickens, and, with parasites present, will often turn opaque white. This is often called white slime disease of the skin.

COSTIA

A single-celled parasite, it is bean- or pear-shaped and has two flagellae (hair-type structures used for locomotion). Costia cling to the fragile mucous membrane of the body of small fish, and feed off the skin, causing damage and leading to haemorrhages and possibly secondary infection by fungus.

Larger fish seem to be unaffected by low levels of infection and often the treatment does more damage than good, but small fish have very low tolerance of this parasite and should be treated as soon as possible.

There are many treatments for costia. Some of the best include:
- A short-term salt bath
- Formalin, either as a bath or as a long-term treatment
- Trypaflavinem as a long bath.

WHITE SPOT

White spot is the best-known fish disease, yet it is rare in cold climates as it does not thrive below 20 degrees Celsius (68 degrees Fahrenheit). The symptoms are white spots the size of sugar grains, which cover the entire body and gills, but are most easily spotted on the fins, where they normally start appearing first.

The fish will become lethargic up to two days before the white spots become visible, and they will scratch on rocks or other objects in the pond. The disease is rarely fatal to large fish but is a major problem for small fish or fry. The adult parasite burrows into the skin and sits under the first layer. Therefore, the treatment cannot affect the adults, only the free-swimming stages of the life cycle.

The best treatments for white spot are:
- **Malachite green:** Used once every five to seven days for three to four treatments.
- **Methylene blue:** A long-term bath for three to five days.
- **Chloramine-T:** Two to three treatments, five to seven days apart. Although very effective, it can cause gill membrane damage to fish of the carp family.

FISH POX

Fish or carp pox is caused by a viral infection, and manifests itself as cream-to-pink waxy lumps on the fins and body. It is seen on koi more than any other fish. It is not particularly infectious and seems to cause no suffering or fish losses. There is no real cure for this problem and so it is best left alone.

Never try to remove the lumps, as this will cause bleeding and an entrance wound leading to bacterial problems. One method to reduce the amounts of pox is to raise the temperature, which will temporarily eliminate the symptoms. However, as soon as the temperature drops, the lumps will reappear. It is said to slow the growth rate of fish but this has not been proven.

Although harmless, it is best to avoid purchasing fish with pox, as it is unsightly, and, on occasions, may spread.

ULCERS

It is almost inevitable that fish will damage themselves at some point in their life, but ulcer disease is a very different problem. Although the ulcer can be started by a bruise, a knock, or by rough handling, it is very infectious and can spread through a pond in days. The main causes are bacteria eating the flesh away, and the fish being unable to fend off the bacteria by themselves.

Nearly all ulcers are caused by poor water quality and high levels of stress. The first visible symptoms are on the front fins, which will start to show the red blood veins, and fish with white skin often show a pink coloration. The fish will often keep feeding, which makes spotting the problem difficult.

It can be caused by any of the following factors, or by a combination of several of them.
- Overpacking during shipping to the retailer or wholesaler.
  In order to keep margins high, some retailers will overpack fish

in order to reduce shipping costs.
- No rest period after shipping. After such a traumatic journey, the fish need to rest for at least two weeks before they are sold on.
- Mixing with other infected fish. Mixing new and old batches of fish, or fish from different countries, is a recipe for disaster.
- Poor water quality. Any extreme can cause sufficient stress or gill damage to give the bacteria a chance to get a hold and for the ulcer to appear. Even high nitrate has been said to cause ulcers.
- Poor diet. Many foods sold lack the necessary vitamins and minerals to support a fish, and, if you also underfeed, the bacteria find the weakened fish an easy target.

If you find an ulcer on a fish, check water quality, find the cause, and remedy it as soon as you can. If possible, isolate the fish, although, by the time the ulcer appears, the disease will have spread already.

Do not increase the temperature quickly, as the bacteria will react faster than the fish, allowing them to overrun the fish's defence systems even more quickly.

Often, fungus will appear as a secondary infection. To avoid this, treat the pond with a fungicide, such as malachite green.

The next step is to identify the bacteria causing the infection. You will need to take a swab from the ulcerated area and send it to a laboratory to have the bacteria cultivated and checked for antibiotic resistance. This should take no more than three to four days. When the results are returned, the correct antibiotic can be used.

If the fish is feeding, use an oral preparation. If not, a course of injections will be needed. It always best to feed if you can, as injecting the fish can lead to a secondary infection. Never treat the pondwater with antibiotics. Finish the course. Just because the fish seem 'fine' does not mean they are fully cured.

To help the healing process, feed a food rich in vitamin C as this helps the skin heal and the immune system to combat disease. Warmer water will also help the healing process, but it must be increased slowly, by no more than 1 degree Celsius per day and no more than 5 degrees Celsius per week. It can take the fish up to two weeks to adjust its metabolic rate to the new temperature, but the bacteria will adjust much quicker. If it is possible to raise the temperature to greater than 22 degrees Celsius (71 degrees Fahrenheit), the fish will heal very quickly.

In the healing process, the skin will to start to grow over the ulcer. A white edge will form around the ulcer and eventually grow right over the wound. Then the scales will start to grow back. Always feed new fresh food high in fish oil and protein to sick or ill fish. It will help to replace energy and provide the protein needed for healing.

TREATMENTS

Generally, it is better to remove the fish from the pond and treat them in a separate tank. This means that, in the event of a miscalculation or problem arising, it is easy to transfer the fish back to a stable, clean environment.

When treating, you need to consider a number of factors that will affect the outcome:

- Do you have the correct diagnosis? Never guess. If you are unsure, seek advice.
- Do you have the volume of the pond/tank correct? This is very important. If you don't know the amount of water, you will not be able to administer the correct dose.
- Are you using the right treatment for the problem? There are many treatments that look similar. Make sure the one you use is designed specifically to cure your problem, otherwise there is a good chance it will not work!
- Do you know the correct treatment level for the chemical? Does the dose make sense? If not, ask your retailer to work it out for you, or contact the manufacturer.
- Is the pond dirty? Any organic matter or soil in the pond will absorb the treatment, so remove them if you can.
- Does the pond have filtration? The filter will break down the chemicals, so adjust the dose as the instructions recommend.
- Remove any chemical absorbents that are present in the filter system, such as carbon and zeolite products.

When using any chemical, always follow the instructions and dose rates that the manufacturer recommends. The fish are unlikely to show an instant response to the treatment but should show signs within a week. If not, reconsider the diagnosis.

Before treating any pond, increase the aeration, as most treatments will reduce the oxygen levels in the water and the fish will suffer. Adding fresh water can also help before treatments, as it often dilutes the 'stale' water. A 15 to 25 per cent water change is ideal.

If the pond is particularly dirty, it will help to vacuum it out before treating, as it not only removes the organic matter but will also remove any parasite eggs or fungal spores that may be lying dormant in the waste. It also reduces the load on the filters.

WORKING OUT THE TREATMENT
The first information you will need is the volume of the pond or tank that you are going to use.

> TIP: *As mentioned elsewhere in this book, when you first build your pond it is advisable to use a water meter as you fill it, so you will always know the volume.*

To calculate the volume, you will need measurements (in metres) of:
- The length of the pond, or average if the end is rounded or uneven
- The width or average
- The depth or average.

With these we can work out the volume as in this example – length 4 metres, width 2.5 metres, depth 0.8 metres. So, 4 x 2.5 x 0.8 = 8 cubic metres. To convert to litres, multiply by 1,000. In this case, the volume would be 8,000 litres. For UK gallons, times cubic metres by 220 (8 x 220 = 1,760 gallons). For US fluid gallons, times cubic metres by 260 (8 x 260 = 2,080 gallons). It is easier to use metric measurements as ready-made treatments are measured out in millilitres (ml) or cubic centimetres (cc).

Round ponds are also easy to work out. You will need measurements (also in metres) of:
- The radius (half the width or diameter)
- The depth or average depth.

The calculation method is radius x radius x 3.14 x depth, which will give your result in cubic metres, as in this example – the pond is 3.5 metres in diameter and 0.75 metres deep. The radius is half the diameter, so 3.5 divided by 2 = 1.75. 1.75 x 1.75 x 3.14 x 0.75 = 7.2 cubic metres, 7.2 x 1000 = 7,200 litres.

Now the volume has been calculated, it is possible to work out how much chemical is required.

HOMEMADE TREATMENTS

Making your own stock treatments can be difficult. The following information can be used as a guide to ensure you use the correct dose for your pond when buying ready-made treatments.

Most of the chemicals can be purchased in solution and are sold separately, enabling the correct mix to be used for each ailment. The ready-mixed treatments are often weak and can lead to the ailment becoming immune or resistant to the treatments.

Remember, chemicals can be very dangerous, not only to the fish, but also to the fishkeeper.

It is highly recommended that gloves and eye protection are worn when handling concentrated chemicals. Many are caustic and contain very strong dyes. **If in doubt, DON'T do it yourself.**

The best way to use concentrated chemicals is to make a stock solution (i.e. diluted to an easy-to-use level).

MAKING A STOCK SOLUTION

This is simply to dilute the chemical to a set dilution, so that you can easily work out how much chemical to use. The more dilute the treatment, the less chance of an overdose.

- To produce a stock solution of 0.1 per cent, add 1 gram of chemical to 1 litre (1,000 ml) of fresh water.
- To produce a stock solution of 1 per cent, add 10 g of chemical to 1 litre (1,000ml) of fresh water.
- To produce a stock solution of 10 per cent, add 100 g of chemical to 1 litre (1,000ml) of fresh water.

All solutions should be stored in the dark in a cool, frost-free dry place away from children and pets. It is best not to keep solutions for more than one year as some of the chemicals degrade and can become toxic. Always dispose of them safely.

CHEMICALS

Many chemicals can be purchased as powders or 50 per cent solutions. Always purchase the best grade, as it will be free from other impurities. Malachite, for example, is often contaminated with zinc, which is very toxic to fish.

The chemicals and doses shown here are only to be used when all the water conditions are within safe levels. If the oxygen level is very low, adding chemicals will lower it still further and may kill the fish.

Always add chemicals in the morning, so that you will have all day to see if a problem occurs. Add half the dose, and, if the fish seem to tolerate it, add the rest 30 to 45 minutes later. Obviously, close observation is important.

ACRIFLAVINE OR TRYPAFLAVINE

An orange powder that is light-sensitive, this is a very strong dye. In water, it is iridescent green and stains just about everything it touches.

Used as a long-term bath for 7 to 10 days at 0.01 mg per litre, it is very good for the treatment of bacterial diseases, such as fin rot, and will kill gill or skin flukes and many other ectoparasites.

At 1g per 100 litres, for two days, it can be used for the control of costia. At these levels, however, it is best not used in a pond, as it may damage plants and biological filters. Treat in a separate tank.

Acriflavine is active until the colour fades.

ALKYL-DIMETHYL-BENZYL-AMMONIUM CHLORIDE OR BENZALKONIUM CHLORIDE (BKC)

This has a very long-winded name, but it is a good and reliable treatment for the early stages of bacterial infections, especially gill and fin rot. It is very strong and can be quite dangerous to young fish.

Normally, it is supplied in 10 or 50 per cent solutions. The recommended rate of use is at 0.02 mg per litre. This will break down in a filtered tank in one to two days, and it can be reapplied every two days for five treatments.

BKC also has a mild detergent effect, and can be used to remove excessive mucus before treating with an anti-parasite product.

Special notes:
- *As BKC has ammonium as part of its make-up, it will be broken down by the biological filter over time.*
- *It is also registered by most ammonia test kits, and can lead to some rather alarming test results. Don't panic.*
- *It will cause surface foaming due to its detergent effect. This is best skimmed off as it will contain fish mucus.*

CHLORAMINE OR CHLORAMINE-T

A white, crystalline powder that breaks down in water very quickly, so it must be used in its powdered form. It is effective against most of the smaller ectoparasites and is quickly absorbed by organic waste so it is best used in clean bare tanks.

For best results, use as a short-term bath for two to four hours at 0.07 mg per litre. It can be used in ponds at 10 gm per 5,000 litres every day for three days.

Special Notes:
- *A face mask must be worn as it irritates the lungs.*
- *It is detrimental to small fish and should not be used on fish measuring less than 10 cm (4 inches) as irreparable gill damage can be caused.*
- *It is not used by many fish farmers as carp do not take the treatment well.*
- *It damages plants and affects biological filters. The more aeration in the pond, the quicker the degrading occurs.*
- *It should not be used with any other chemicals. It is a bleaching compound and discolours most material.*

COPPER SULPHATE

A very dangerous chemical in the pond environment as it is very toxic at low levels. Unless everything else has failed, it is best to avoid using copper sulphate, but it is a very effective treatment for costia, ectoparasites, fungus and oodinium. Young fish are intolerant of copper sulphate and should be treated at a different dose (see below).
- **Treatment one:** The safest way to treat fish is in a bath of 1 g per 10 litres of water for no more than 20 minutes. For longer term and lower doses, a stock solution of 1 g per litre should be made up for ease of application.

- **Treatment two:** A long-term bath of 2 ml (of stock solution) per 1 litre for 7 to 10 days.
- **Treatment three (for young fish):** Young fish can be treated at 0.5 ml (of stock solution) per litre of water for 15 seconds to 1 minute.

Start at the shortest time first and work up, until the treatment is successful.

Special notes:
- *Copper sulphate is toxic to all fish at relatively low levels, but some fish, such as sturgeon, sterlet, tench and catfish, are not tolerant to it at any level. If you are unsure* don't use it.
- *It will kill all plants at the levels shown above and should not be used in ponds.*
- *Always treat in a separate tank and have plenty of water available to do a water change if necessary.*

FORMALIN OR FORMALDEHYDE

More often than not, this is used in conjunction with malachite green for the treatment of ectoparasites. It is effective against flukes, trichodina and white spot. It can be used as a short-term bath or a long-term pond treatment.

Formalin or formaldehyde is normally purchased as a 35 or 37 per cent solution. For mild parasite infections, use 1 ml per 65 litres of water (15 ml per cubic metre or 1,000 litres), and, for stubborn cases, use 1 ml per 40 litres (25 ml per cubic metre or 1,000 litres).

For short-term treatments, 1 ml per 4 litres can be used as a bath for 25 to 40 minutes. The fish should be placed in the bath in a net so that it can be removed quickly if necessary and without any personal contact with the solution.

Caution: This dose is very dangerous and should only be used as a last resort, and never in a pond.

Special notes:
- *Formalin is very toxic and forms a vapour that is extremely unpleasant. It is very caustic and burns skin, eyes and lungs, so it should only be used in a well-ventilated area and with appropriate protection – gloves, goggles and a face-mask.*

- *It deoxygenates the water very quickly and extra aeration should be used at all times.*
- *Young fish should not be treated as they will suffer gill damage.*
- *Some species will suffer fin and gill damage at very low levels. If unsure, use the lowest dose first.*
- *In areas of soft water, formalin is more toxic than in hard water so adjust the dose accordingly.*
- *If left for a time, formalin will form white crystals on the base of the container. If this happens, dispose of the whole bottle as the crystals are very toxic.*

MALACHITE GREEN

The best-known chemical for the treatment of fungi, bacterial infections and external parasites. Its best use is for the treatment of parasites, as a continuous bath for 10 to 14 days. During the treatment, it needs to be added three times to make sure all the parasites are treated as they hatch.

For a long-term bath, a level of 0.1 to 0.2 mg per litre is required (1 to 2 ml of 1 per cent stock solution per 100 litres of water). For short-term baths, a level of 1 to 2mg per litre for 45 to 60 minutes is required (1 to 2 ml of 1 per cent stock solution per 10 litres of water).

Before any treatments with malachite, the pond must be cleaned of all sludge or accumulated organic waste, as it will deactivate the malachite quickly, leaving the treatment incomplete.

Special notes:
- *If the powder form is purchased, it must be zinc-free, as zinc is very toxic to fish.*
- *It is a strong dye and colours everything blue.*
- *It is thought to be carcinogenic (cancer-causing) so gloves and eye protection must be worn.*
- *It can be neutralised with bleach (but not in a pond).*
- *It forms crystals if the solution becomes cold, but this is safe, and, when the solution is warmed up, the crystals will dissolve again.*

MALACHITE AND FORMALIN COMBINATION

The most common ready-to-use combination for ponds. The mixture of malachite green and formalin has all the properties of both chemicals and is very effective when used as a long-term treatment for external parasites and fungus infections. It can be purchased ready-mixed, although more dilute than the 'proper' mix.

The normal mix made for use is 3.7 g of zinc-free malachite green powder in 1 litre of 37 per cent formalin solution. This is then used at 1 ml per 40 litres. It is a very strong treatment, and care should be taken when using this mixture.

POTASSIUM PERMANGANATE

Sold as purple crystals, potassium permanganate is useful in fishkeeping because it can be used on fish that are sensitive to organophosphate treatments. It is also one of the few treatments that works on fish lice. Use as a bath for 30 minutes only at a concentration of 20 mg per litre (20 ml of a 1 per cent stock solution per litre of water).

Undissolved crystals must never be added to the water containing fish as they will kill them. The crystals must be dissolved and then left for 30 to 60 minutes before use. It is quickly deactivated by organic matter and best used in a separate treatment tank.

Special notes:
Potassium permanganate is a strong dye and oxidiser. It discolours most materials, including clothes and stonework. It also stains skin brown. Gloves and face protection should be worn.

ORGANOPHOSPHATES (TRICHLORFON, NALED®, AND DIPTREX®)

Some of the most dangerous chemicals adopted by the fish industry. They are insecticides, which act by damaging the nervous system. It has to be said that these chemicals are effective, but I believe they should be avoided as they are very toxic and can permanently affect humans.

SODIUM CHLORIDE (COMMON SALT)

The only salt to use is pure salt. There must be no additives, such as iodine, although an anticaking agent is fine. The best types to use are cooking salt or pure vacuum-dried salt (often called PVD).

Salt is one of the safest treatments. Fish show obvious signs of distress by 'falling over' in the water if they can no longer tolerate the treatment. They can then be removed into pond water and usually recover quickly, without any major damage. Salt can be used to treat almost any complaint, from minor bacterial skin infections to parasites.

Salt is useful in helping fish recover from bacterial infections, not so much as a direct treatment but because salt reduces the fish's water uptake. Therefore the fish expends less energy on ridding itself of excess water and more energy on healing itself. This process is called osmoregulation. As pond fish live in fresh water, they absorb water from the surroundings by osmosis, a process that allows water to travel from a low concentration (the pond water) to a higher concentration (the blood), through a semi-permeable membrane (the surface of the gills). Freshwater fish also lose salts to the pond water by diffusion and use valuable energy in recovering them. Any factor that affects these biological processes reduces the energy required by the fish. This allows the fish to use the energy more effectively for body repairs.

To aid recovery and repairs from damage, a salt level of 2 g per litre, as a long-term bath, can be used for periods of up to six months without any ill effects.

The use of salt to treat parasites relies on the process of osmosis. The stronger salt solution 'draws' water from the parasites faster than they can replace it and, because of this, they dehydrate to a point where they die. As the fish can stand much higher levels of salt than the parasites, it does not have such an effect on them and they recover from the treatment.

For short-term baths to kill parasites, levels of 20 g per litre for 10 to 20 minutes can be used safely. The smaller the fish, the shorter the time should be, as they will be affected to a greater extent than larger fish.

Treatment levels of up to 60 g per litre have been used in very difficult cases but only for very short periods of time (two minutes or less) as they can kill the fish very easily.

Special notes:
- *Although salt is a very safe treatment and even overdosing can be 'safe' for the fish, it is always best to treat fish in a tank, and any water left over must be diluted and disposed of down a drain. It will kill any plants or lawn it comes into contact with.*

- *Almost any level of salt will affect pond plants, so introduction in a planted pond is a recipe for disaster.*
- *The use of a background salt level in non-planted ponds to act as a preventative treatment is not a good idea, for the following reasons:*
  - *Salt lowers the oxygen-holding capacity of water.*
  - *The filter will not be as effective, as less oxygen in the water will affect the bacteria too.*
  - *It lowers the freezing point of water, which will lead to colder water in the winter and possible loss of fish.*
  - *It affects plant growth and, at low levels, kills plants.*
  - *Salt water is not a natural medium for freshwater fish. It does not help them if they are healthy.*
  - *Any background level will help the parasites to become immune to the salt's effect.*
  - *Salt will make the ammonia more toxic than at the same level in fresh water.*

ANTIBIOTICS

Antibiotic use in the consumer fish market leaves a lot to be desired. More resistant strains of bacteria have appeared than in almost any other area where antibiotics are used. I have not suggested or recommended any antibiotics by name or group, as it is imperative that the correct one be used or, not only will the fish die, but the bacteria could become resistant to the treatment.

Quite often, in a pond that is warm, with good water quality and a plentiful food supply, the fish will heal themselves of all but the worst infections. The more you handle the fish, the more stress they will suffer and the sicker they may become.

The expert who suggests an antibiotic for the treatment of a fish must know the answers to all the following questions:

- Have the fish been tested to see which antibiotic will cure the problem?
- Has any other problem caused the outbreak? If so, it needs curing first.
- Have any other antibiotics been used in the pond before?

It may seem obvious, but the most common error that kills fish is the misuse of remedies. There is no point treating with antibiotic 'A' if the disease is not affected by or is resistant to it. Therefore, it is common sense to get a fish autopsied, if it has died, or a scrape done. Once the culture has been taken, the lab can give you a result in a few days that will give you the chance to save the rest of the fish quickly and safely.

Remember, in most cases, the cause of an infection can be traced to poor water quality or damage from rough handling. If this problem is not cured first, then the fish will become ill again from the environmental conditions. If the fish have been treated before with an antibiotic, there is a good chance that any antibiotic from the same family will not work.

The method of treatment can have as much to do with the healing process as the treatment itself. The quickest and easiest method is to mix the antibiotic with food and feed the fish for the whole period of the treatment. This has a number of advantages. The first is that the fish can be left in the pond without disturbing the fish or its companions.

A blanket treatment is not the best method but it will cover those fish in which illness has gone undetected. It is easy to administer and requires little technical know-how, making the chance of the course completion more likely. The disadvantage is that all the fish have to be fed and therefore more antibiotic must be used. Also, not all the fish will get the correct dose.

The second method is to inject each fish. This is fine if only a small number of fish need treating, and it guarantees the correct dose for each fish. But it has a number of major drawbacks.

Whenever a fish is anaethetised, it is at risk and some of the anaesthetics cause irreparable damage to the liver. The injection makes another entry point for bacteria, and the use of dirty needles leads to secondary infection. This is a very common problem, often characterised by an ulcer at the injection site.

Injections must be done at set times to ensure the treatment is completed, but, in fish, the temperature is also a major factor. The warmer the water, the shorter the time between injections. Also, as the injection can give quicker results, the course is often stopped early because the fish appears to have recovered. Unfortunately, this is seldom the case and the bacteria then become immune to the antibiotic when treatment is recommenced.

The point of injection is also a problem. The best position is into a muscle either in the pectoral fin or the tail. Other suitable places include the body cavity, but the chance of damaging internal organs is high and this area has a low blood flow, so the spread around the body is slow.

NB: An injection should only be done by a competent, qualified, specialist veterinarian.

The last method is to bathe the fish in water with an antibiotic dissolved in it. Some of the newer antibiotics are not very soluble and this can cause problems. The solution will also become toxic after a short period as the antibiotic 'goes off.' It also kills filter bacteria, so any solution that makes its way into the pond can cause more problems than it solves. The uptake by the fish is very variable, and so its effectiveness can be unreliable.

Golden rules for the use of antibiotics:

- Whatever antibiotic you use, always finish the course.
- Never mix antibiotics, unless recommended by the manufacturer.
- Never use antibiotics intended for humans on fish.
- Always get the right one for the job. Never guess.

If in doubt, get a qualified (not self-appointed) person to check the fish for you.

CHAPTER 13

ALGAE

Algae is the most common problem encountered by fishkeepers and is possibly the hardest to cure permanently. Algae plant thrives in a well-lit pond with plenty of nutrients, so it is nearly always a summer problem, and the increase in temperature at this time of year only compounds it.

As algae can multiply very quickly, it generally outperforms and outgrows the normal pond plants. In many cases, it will kill off submerged plants by cutting out the light. It can also lead to lack of oxygen at night, especially in warmer weather when oxygen levels are normally low anyway.

There are two main algae growths – green water and stringy 'blanket weed'. Normally, if you have green water, blanket weed does not grow well, as there is no sunlight, but if you have clear water then the blanket weed will grow instead.

COPING WITH ALGAE

There are many options for the removal of algae from ponds. The most common mistake made by pondkeepers is to empty the green pond and refill with fresh water. This will start the process all over again, as the introduction of fresh water means that new nutrients have been made available – more food for the algae.

CHEMICALS AND HERBICIDES

The quickest and easiest way to remove algae is to add chemicals. Some dye the algae, which inhibits its growth and it soon dies. Some are aquatic herbicides which, at low levels, only affect algae. However, there is always a danger to other pond plants, particularly water lilies.

A natural method, such as balancing the number of fish against the plants, does work, but very slowly. Another natural control of algae has been the production of plant extracts, the most common being barley straw. It is available as natural barley straw pads, which are placed in the pond so that they can rot down, and the enzyme that affects the algae is released. The whole process can take up to six weeks to start working and the pads need to be added well before the main algae season starts in the spring. As the straw rots away, new pads need to be added before the old ones run out, to keep the cycle going.

Barley straw extract is also sold as a ready-to-use liquid containing the enzyme. It needs to be added every month and it is not generally as effective as the straw itself. The only drawback with any of the chemical additives, man-made or natural, is that they do not work in every pond, and may not even work from one year to the next, as the algae slowly becomes immune to the chemicals.

When using chemicals, it is essential that you follow the instructions very carefully. As the algae starts to die, it will pollute and deoxygenate the water, which can lead to fish deaths. Follow a few simple tips to avoid any problems.

- Make sure the pond pump is running at its highest setting. This will create extra oxygenation and pump the water through the filter quicker, thus filtering out the worse of the dead algae.
- Clean the pump regularly during treatment, as it will clog with the free-floating dead algae.
- Put a fine filter mat in the filter. This will collect the dead algae quicker, and it can be washed every day without upsetting the biological section of the filter, or clogging it up.

- Reduce the amount of food you give to your fish. This will reduce the amount of oxygen they require and lower the load on the filter, as they will produce less waste.
- Once the pond has cleared, vacuum the dead algae from the bottom of the pond to stop the nutrients re-entering the cycle. Proprietary sludge-removing products may also help.

ULTRAVIOLET AND ELECTRONIC METHODS

One of the most reliable methods of controlling green water is the use of an ultraviolet clarifier. This is a method that has proved its worth for many years and is the best long-term cure for the condition. It is installed with a biological filter and pump, and needs to run 24 hours a day, seven days a week, to get the best results (see chapter six).

The control of blanket weed with electronic devices is more difficult. None of the products I have tried has proved very reliable, and those that work only do so for a very short period of time. Algae adapts to its new surroundings very quickly and soon nullifies the effect of the electronics.

You can also buy a permanent magnet that is placed in the pumped water line. This has a similar effect to the electronic devices and is about as effective. It will last longer if you remove it when it appears to stop working and start again in three or four months' time.

The only way to find out if these devices will work for you is to try them. Some do, most do not.

VEGETABLE FILTERS

The best and most reliable method for getting rid of green water and blanket weed is to use plants. It costs nothing to run and improves the water quality at the same time.

The basic principle is to use plants to consume the excess nutrients before the algae can get to them. A simple plant filter is called a 'vegetable filter'. It is a very basic form of hydroponics, and uses water plants to remove the nutrients from the water in order to grow. The best plants to use are the ones that will grow fastest in the prevailing conditions. Watercress *(Nastridium sp.)* is very good. Not only does it grow very quickly, it also uses up a very large amount of nitrogen in the process. It can also be fed to the fish.

The vegetable filter's design is very simple. It requires little maintenance and works very well. The best position for the filter is in full sun, as the plants will do better with more light. It is best placed after the bio filter to take advantage of the highest concentration of nitrate, a plant food, because the bio filter converts the fish waste to nitrate (see page 122).

The filter needs to be shallow, with a gravel substrate that the plants can root into but no soil, as this will stop the plants doing their job. The slower the water flows through the filter, the better, as the plants will have more time to extract the nutrients.

As this section of the filter has a lot of plants in it, protection from koi will be needed or they will destroy it. If you have no room for a separate vegetable filter, then it is possible to grow water plants in a waterfall or even in the top of the bio filter.

USING A WATERFALL AS A VEGI-FILTER

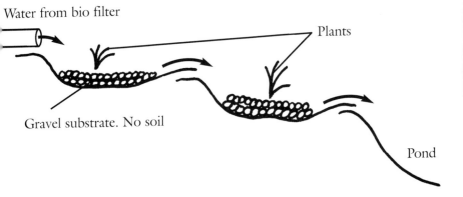

The vegetable filter method can take time to start working, but do not be tempted to use chemicals to help, as they will certainly affect the plants you want to grow. If the need for an 'instant' cure is important, the addition of floating plants will help to speed things up. They not only use the nutrients to grow, but also block the light from the algae, and they can be thinned and removed as necessary.

FISH CARE

Whatever you decide to use to control algae, bear in mind that the main cause of it is the fish. The more fish you have, the more waste they will produce, and the more algae will grow.

It must be remembered that the reason the algae is growing is because nature is trying to reduce the toxic waste levels in the pond before they can harm the fish. The growth of algae should be taken as a good thing as it is saving your fish. All that is needed is to replace the algae with another plant that is more manageable and easier to control.

CHAPTER 14

POND MAINTENANCE

Regular maintenance is the only way to keep on top of any problems. It should be a pleasure, not a chore. Simple daily maintenance need only be a check that the fish are swimming and the pump is working. This can be done while you are feeding your fish each day.

SPRING

Spring is the pondkeeper's busiest time of the year. This is the best time to replace bog and marginal plants that have died. Overgrown plants can be taken out, divided, and repotted ready for the new season. Clean the paving, without using chemicals, and remove any winter debris such as leaves.

The pump and pipework should be checked for frost damage, cleaned and tested. The filter and ultraviolet units should be checked for leaks and any failed bulbs should be replaced. The filter should be allowed to run for a few weeks before the ultraviolet filter is turned on, so that the bacteria can re-establish themselves.

Check fish for signs of disease and treat when water is warmer than 10 degrees Celsius (50 degrees Fahrenheit). Start feeding the fish when the temperature is greater than 5 degrees Celsius (41 degrees Fahrenheit), giving small amounts at first.

Remove the fine net that was put over the pond to protect it from autumn/winter leaves, and replace it with a coarser net to stop predators attacking the fish.

Spring is the best time to clean out the pond and carry out any major rebuilding. A complete empty and refill should not be necessary every year, unless excessive leaf-fall fills the pond in the autumn (fall).

SUMMER

Time to weed and dead-head self-seeding plants, cut back invasive plants, add new plants and water lilies. Add feed to new plants to help establish them and encourage good growth. Watch out for pests on the plants, as you cannot spray them because of the fish. Remove infected leaves or wash off with a strong water jet.

Remove algae as it grows, and, in the case of blanket weed, try adding barley straw to suppress the growth. Trim oxygenators as they grow to encourage new, more vigorous growth.

Check your pump pre-filter and clean as necessary. The foams in the bio filter will also need cleaning on a regular basis.

Feed the fish more frequently, with two or three small feeds a day. Add new fish, but remember to quarantine them first. During thundery weather, keep the pump running to avoid low oxygen levels killing the fish, or add an air pump as a back-up.

AUTUMN (FALL)

Cut back hard all submerged plants to avoid them dying in the winter and polluting the pond. Remove all rotting material from the pond and cut away leaves and stalks from marginals. Remove any tender plants you have added in summer and overwinter in frost-free conditions.

Feed your fish well to ready them for the winter hibernation ahead. When the fish have stopped feeding in late autumn or early winter (depending on the temperature), drain the filters and remove ultraviolet systems to store indoors. Clean the pump and remove if necessary. Cover your pond with a fine net to catch leaves and stop animals falling in.

WINTER

The fish should stop feeding as the temperature drops to 5 degrees Celsius (41 degrees Fahrenheit) or below and will not require feeding again until spring. Cover any tender plants with old leaves or straw to protect them from frost. In very severe weather, you will need to create a hole in the ice to let toxic gases escape and to stop the ice expanding and damaging the edging of the pond. In a normal winter, a floating ball or plastic container will prevent ice forming, but, in very cold weather, a floating electric heater may be required.

Do not use a pump, as this will mix the warmer water on the bottom of the pond with the colder water at the surface. This can make small ponds freeze completely in very cold weather.

ALL-YEAR-ROUND MAINTENANCE

The table on the page overleaf is a guide to water gardening all year round.

As with any gardening project, the temperature is the main factor. If it is very warm, there is always work to be done, and, when it is cold and the fish are hibernating, it is time to go indoors and relax.

With the average pond, the work involved takes no more than one hour a week, but things can and do go wrong. Keep a few spares for your pump, such as filters and an impeller. If you are in a rush, you will be able to swap filters and clean the other one later. A spare pump is a must if you have a large collection of fish.

The most important advice is to do maintenance frequently, as it will not involve too much time or effort. Remember, little and often always pays off.

SEASONAL MAINTENANCE

Time	Fish	Plants	Water	Work & accessories
Spring	Start to feed fish when temperature reaches 5°C (41°C). Watch for diseases.	Divide overgrown plants and repot. Add new oxygenators and marginals.	Check water quality.	Remove net. Set up filter. Check pump and pipework. Now is the time to start new projects.
Summer	Feed regularly. Watch for spawning. Remove fry to a growing pond. Put non-hardy fish in pond.	Cut back excess growth and plant new lilies and marginals. Add non-hardy floating plants	Top up pond as necessary and check water regularly. Check oxygen levels.	Clean filter as needed. Clean pump and fountain heads frequently.
Autumn (Fall)	Feed up for winter. Watch temperature. Move any non-hardy fish indoors.	Cut back excess growth and dead-head flowers.	Check water.	Remove excess leaves as they fall.
Winter	Stop feeding below 5 degrees Celsius (41°F).	Remove old growth and floating plants.	Watch for ice damage.	Net pond. Install heater.

CHAPTER 15

CLEANING OUT
THE POND

One of the most commonly asked questions by water gardeners is 'When should I clean my out my pond?' There is no hard-and-fast rule, as all ponds differ. Smaller ponds generally require more maintenance than larger ones. The addition of filtration will reduce the need to clean, as material will be removed during regular maintenance. If a particular species of plant regularly outgrows the pond, the obvious answer is to replace it with a slow-growing, smaller species.

A quick check to see whether the pond needs cleaning is to run a net across the bottom. If the net is full of half-rotted leaves and silt, you will know it needs doing.

The build-up of rubbish and waste in the pond is due to the liner. In a natural pond, any plant material that fell to the bottom would rot and turn into soil. The nutrients released would be used in new plant growth. Unfortunately, the liner in a man-made pond inhibits this process, which, in turn, increases the speed at which sludge accumulates on the bottom. The more sludge there is, the higher the oxygen demand by the bacteria to break it down. This can pose problems during warm weather, as oxygen levels can fall dangerously low, leading to unexplained fish deaths. It is important, therefore, to keep the waste levels as low as possible to avoid this.

Another reason for cleaning out the pond is to remove excess fish. Many ponds become overstocked, and reducing the numbers not only relieves pressure on the pond and filtration, but also reduces stress and increases the fishes' ability to resist disease.

The best time to clean the pond is in early spring, before frogs and other animals come to spawn, or in late autumn (fall) after the frost has stopped the plants growing. Only clean the pond in summer in an emergency, as the warmer weather can lead to disaster when the fish are put in a holding tank.

PREPARATION

Cleaning your pond is a major undertaking and will take more time than you anticipate. There is always more work to do then you can see. These are the items you will need:

- Pump and pipework
- Net to catch fish
- Clean bucket
- Water conditioner
- Holding tank (It should be large enough to hold all the fish from the pond. Dustbins are not ideal, as they have a very small surface area and this could cause fish losses due to lack of oxygen.)
- Dustpan and brush
- Garden hose to refill pond
- New planting baskets, aquatic soil, gravel and fertiliser
- Sharp knife
- Line repair kit in case of any accidents.

CLEANING

Set a holding tank up in the shade well away from the pond. Pump the pond water into the holding tank until it is half-filled, then top the rest up with water from the tap (faucet) and water conditioner. This will acclimatise the fish to new water.

As the holding tank is filling, remove all planted baskets, allowing the fish to escape into deeper water as the level reduces. Check each

> *Tip: Do not pump muddy water down the household drain as it may block it. Pump the water on to a flowerbed. The water will soak in, leaving the mud and waste on the surface, which can be then dug in as a fertiliser.*

basket for any fish that may have become caught up in the roots.

Once the pond is half-empty, the rest of the water can be pumped to waste. Never leave the pump running without supervision in case it pumps the pond dry and leaves the fish without water.

Catch the fish as the water level recedes and transfer to a bucket of pond water. Any mud or sediment that has stuck to the fish will then be washed off. When you have caught all the fish, carry them over to the holding tank and carefully tip, though not from a great height.

Install a small water or air pump to oxygenate the holding tank while you clean the pond, covering the holding tank with a net cover. This will stop fish jumping out, and will reduce stress by restricting the amount of light in the tank.

Before entering the pond, make sure there are no stones or sharp edges to the shoes or boots you are wearing, as this could damage the liner. Once the pond is empty, use the dustpan and brush to remove any stones and sludge from the pond. Hose down the pond with fresh water and pump it to waste. This is a good time to fix any loose paving or rockery stones that may have become loose.

Once all remedial work has been done, refill the pond with fresh water. Place the hose in the pond with a garden spray on the end, which will help to warm the water and disperse any chlorine that may be present. Add the correct amount of water conditioner to a bucket of water and stir until well dispersed. This can then be tipped into the pond.

REPOTTING PLANTS

Remove any overgrown plants from the baskets with a sharp knife, cutting away the roots on the outside. Do this away from the pond in case you drop the knife and damage the liner. Once this is accomplished, it should be possible to remove the plant and root ball from the basket without damaging it. With older plants, reduce the height of the foliage by two-thirds and then cut the roots back to half their length.

Before re-using the baskets, hose off all rubbish and debris. This will also wash away any snail eggs. Remove any old flower stalks and divide the plants into smaller clumps. Always keep the youngest plants.

Next, replant them in the newly cleaned pond baskets with a good-quality aquatic soil, and top off with 2 to 3 cm (1 to 1.5 inches) of aquatic gravel. Water the baskets before placing back into the pond. This will wash away any excess soil and should help to keep the pond a little bit cleaner.

Do not overplant, but keep any spare plants in a frost-free place in case any of the newly potted plants do not make it. Remember to leave gaps behind the baskets for the fish to swim through.

CLEANING PUMPS AND FILTERS

As most ponds include pumps and filters, it is advisable to clean them at the same time. The pump should be taken apart in accordance with the manufacturer's instructions, and all parts cleaned with fresh water.

Replace any rings or seals that have cracked or become damaged, and check the impeller. These replacement parts will be available from your local aquatic retailer.

The filter can be cleaned by removing all the media and rinsing with fresh water. The biological filter media should be washed with pond water to avoid killing the bacteria that are growing on them.

You should also clean the pipework, because if this clogs, it dramatically reduces the pump's efficiency and output. Thread a small piece of string through the pipe at one end, attaching a piece of sponge or cloth that will just fit into the pipe. Pull this through the pipework, then rinse out the pipe. Do this two to three more times, until no more waste material is displaced.

VACUUMING THE POND

The advent of cheap pond vacuums has reduced the frequency of complete pond cleans. Regular vacuuming not only benefits the pond but reduces pump and filter maintenance. There will be less algae growth, and less chance of fish disease and parasite infections.

CHAPTER 16

WATER FEATURES AND FOUNTAINS

The building techniques shown in this book can be applied to any water feature, of any size. Many features can now be bought as ready-to-go units, and all you need to add is the water. This section of the book will show some designs that can be adjusted to your site and budget.

MILLSTONE FOUNTAIN

Originally made with real millstones, many are now constructed from cast stone and even fibre glass. To make one you will require:

• A millstone (or any water garden ornament)
• A sump (either a ready-made one, or pond liner plus underlay)
• A pump
• Hose and clip
• Cobbles for decoration.

The first task is to dig out the area for the sump. It needs to hold about 50 litres (11 UK gallons or 13 US fluid gallons). The hole must be at least 40 cm (15 inches) deep in the centre, with a sloping, shallow surround to channel the water back to the sump. The hole can then be fitted out with underlay and liner, or a ridged pre-formed pebble pool liner, which will need sand to bed it in.

The pump and hose need to be connected to the millstone, which can then be lowered over the sump. Make sure there is a gap between the millstone and liner to allow the water to flow back into the sump. If it is tight, rest the millstone on some thin pieces of stone or house bricks. Put underlay beneath the bricks to stop them damaging the liner. The millstone needs to be level to get an even flow over the edges. It can be skimmed if necessary to level it. The cobbles can then be placed around the edge to hide the liner.

MILLSTONE

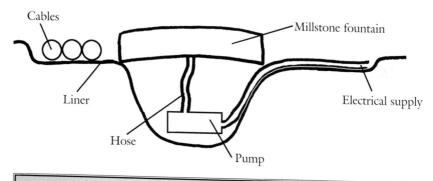

> *Tip: It is easier to level if it is supported in three places only.*

The water level will go down quickly in summer, so turn the pump off at night and top up with water regularly. Use an algaecide to control algae growth on the millstone.

WALL FEATURE

Another feature that is easy to set up is the wall feature. You will require:

- A container for the pond (either a ready-made one, half a wooden water butt, or pond liner plus underlay)
- A pump with hose and clip (if the pipe is to run up the wall and be visible, use copper pipe – it will look better and be easier to fix)

- An ornament to hang on the wall
- Water plants for the pool.

The pool at the base of the wall can be bricked around to hide the ready-made unit or to hold the liner in place, in the same way as a raised pond. If you are unable to drill the wall to run your pipe up the back, run copper pipework up the front of the wall. The ornament should be fixed to the wall as the manufacturer instructs. Make sure it is secure as it will damage the pool and pump if it falls down. Flexible hose can be attached to the pump and to the copper tube, and from the copper tube to the ornament. Once filled, it will be ready to go.

The pool can be planted with water plants that will help to control the algae. Unless the pool is deep, it will not be suitable for fish, as such a small volume of water will suffer extremes of temperature.

SIMPLE WATERFALL FEATURE

A simple, recirculating waterfall feature can be built in an afternoon. You will need:

- A pre-formed waterfall section
- A sump (either a liner or a large bucket/dustbin)
- Mesh to cover the sump
- A pump hose and clip
- Cobbles or rocks to cover the sump.

Dig the hole for the sump and fit in. Fit the waterfall so that it overhangs the sump. Connect the hose to the pump with a clip and install the pump into the sump, running the hose to the top of the waterfall. Place the mesh over the sump and cover with the cobbles or rocks. Fill with water, and away you go.

The pre-formed waterfall can be replaced with a stream section, or you can even make your own with liner and stonework. The designs are endless. Only your imagination and budget will restrict the final size and layout.

FOUNTAINS

Fountains not only provide decoration but also serve other useful purposes, such as creating gentle background noise in an otherwise quiet wildlife pond, and increasing oxygenation during the hot summer months.

With the advent of modern materials and production techniques, the patterns available have increased dramatically and become even more affordable. Unlike filtration pumps, fountain pumps must incorporate a strainer to stop particles being pumped into the fountain head and clogging the nozzles. This difference can make the choice of pump difficult, as both features are at opposite ends of the range. The best option is to use two pumps – one to run the fountain, and one to run the filter system. This not only gives you a back-up, in case one fails, but also the option of not running the fountain if the weather is too windy or cold.

Fountain pumps also need to pump the water at high pressure in order to give the fountain height. When selecting a fountain, always check to make sure that the pump can give the height that you require. Most manufacturers provide a table showing each pump model and its maximum height with each fountain head.

Choosing the fountain nozzle can be difficult enough, but there are a few other factors to consider before purchasing one.

- Most water plants do not like water splashing on to their leaves, as they will be scorched in the sun.
- Fountains increase water evaporation in small ponds. This can be a problem if you go on holiday for a long time.
- The fountain height must never be more than half the width of the pond, as strong winds will blow the falling water outside of the pond and drain it.
- The fountain design needs to fit the pond. A tiered fountain in a natural pond will look out of place, but a small bubbling fountain would look like a spring and fit right in.
- If fish provide the main source of interest and the fountain disturbs the water surface all the time, you won't see them.
- Look for stainless steel or brass nozzles, as they are easier to clean and will last longer.

You will need to get at the pump for maintenance, so raise it off the pond base. This will also help to reduce cleaning, as the pump will be out of the debris. The addition of a large, foam pre-filter will also help, and it will protect the fountain head from material that clogs the jets.

WATER FOUNTAIN

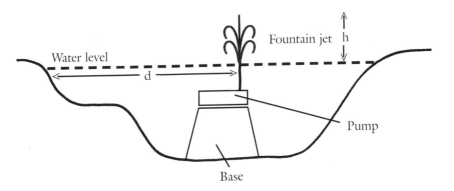

d = half pond's minimum width

h = height of fountain

In some ponds the addition of a fountain will cause a white/cream-coloured foam to appear around the base of the nozzle. This is a protein scum, and it should be removed by skimming it off with a bucket. If it persists, the installation of a surface skimmer will cure the problem.

> *Note: While it is possible to reduce the foam with a chemical antifoaming agent, this will merely hide the problem, not cure it.*

The more complex the fountain pattern, the more likely it will be to clog. If you do not have the time for regular maintenance, look for a more informal fountain, such as a geyser or water bell, as the larger jet openings will not block as quickly.

IMPORTANT TIPS

When constructing any water feature, it is imperative that all electrical work is carried out properly. If you are unsure, get a qualified person to install it.

Most features that involve a small volume of water will suffer algae problems, so the use of algaecides will almost certainly be necessary. If you want to include plants in the feature, you will need to use natural algaecides, which are plant-friendly.

Water will be lost to evaporation quickly, so it is best to use a timer to turn the pump off when you are not around and at night. This will save the pump if the water runs out. Always use a low-maintenance pump, as it will be difficult to get at, once installed.